"Writing powerful, compelling, edge-of-t[...] the things Neill D. Hicks does well. Anot[...] valuable experience, and insight on to [...] want to know how to structure dynamic, exciting films for the global market."

> — **Gloria Stern**
> Author, *Do The Write Thing: Making the Transition To Professional;* Founder, The Gloria Stern Literary Agency

"This is NOT a book just for writers. It is a book for people who have an interest in, and want to know more about, the Thriller genre. And by "more" I don't mean plot points, formulas, and examples calculated to stress those points. This book takes an almost physical grasp of the thread between the audience and the story and gives it a good, hard yank."

> — **Sable Jak**
> *Scr(I)pt Magazine*

"With numerous script excerpts in a screenwriting book that breaks new ground, Neill Hicks demonstrates how the screenwriter may exploit these subliminal audience psychodynamics to craft a powerful screenplay."

> — From the Foreword by Martin Blinder, M.D., Professor of Clinical Psychiatry, University of California, San Francisco

MICHAEL WIESE PRODUCTIONS
www.mwp.com

Since 1981, Michael Wiese Productions has been dedicated to providing novice and seasoned filmmakers with vital information on all aspects of filmmaking and videomaking. We have published more than 60 books, used in over 500 film schools worldwide.

Our authors are successful industry professionals — they believe that the more knowledge and experience they share with others, the more high-quality films will be made. That's why they spend countless hours writing about the hard stuff: budgeting, financing, directing, marketing, and distribution. Many of our authors, including myself, are often invited to conduct filmmaking seminars around the world.

We truly hope that our publications, seminars, and consulting services will empower you to create enduring films that will last for generations to come.

We're here to help. Let us hear from you.

Sincerely,

Michael Wiese
Publisher, Filmmaker

WRITING THE
THRILLER
FILM

THE TERROR WITHIN

NEILL D. HICKS

Published by Michael Wiese Productions
11288 Ventura Blvd., Suite 621
Studio City, CA 91604
tel. (818) 379-8799
fax (818) 986-3408
mw@mwp.com
www.mwp.com

Cover Design: Art Hotel
Book layout: Objects of Design
Editor: Brett Jay Markel

Printed by McNaughton & Gunn, Inc., Saline, Michigan
Manufactured in the United States of America

©2002 Neill D. Hicks

Library of Congress Cataloging-in-Publication Data
Hicks, Neill D., 1946-
      Writing the thriller film : the terror within/
      by Neill D. Hicks.
       p. cm.
      ISBN 0-941188-39-6
      1. Adventure films--History and criticism. 2. Suspense in motion pictures.
      3. Motion picture authorship. I. Title.
      PN1995.9.A3 H53 2002
      791.43'655--dc21

                      2002008550
                         CIP

TABLE OF CONTENTS

BY
MARTIN BLINDER, M.D.
Professor of Clinical Psychiatry
University of California, San Francisco

A movie succeeds to the extent that its audience identifies with the film's protagonist (and often with its *antagonist* as well); unconsciously, those sitting in the theater ought to see themselves on the screen — not a physical likeness but a projection of who they are inside and the immutable psychological issues with which they, like all of us, must grapple.

As Neill Hicks makes clear:

The Romantic Comedy will work to the extent that we all want to win the heart of our archetypal idealized lover.

The Action-Adventure flick will win us over to the extent that it enables each of us to vicariously beat the daylights out of some introjected composite of all the nasty people in our lives who have pushed us around.

And the Thriller grips us best when — by proxy, through the hero — we meet, are initially overwhelmed by, but mature and grow sufficient to enable us to subdue some primordial fear.

With numerous script excerpts in a screenwriting book that breaks new ground, Neill demonstrates how the screenwriter may exploit these subliminal audience psychodynamics to craft a powerful screenplay, digging beneath the surface of writing technique to plumb its psychological underpinnings. In this text his focus is the Thriller, whose heretofore innocent, somewhat detached protagonist finds his life in peril while at the same moment he is abruptly cut off from all his usual support systems (which may, in fact, betray him). Now utterly alone, in Act III he discovers — or creates — new resources within himself: strengths, aptitudes, and a moral resolve heretofore inconceivable. Over the course of two movie hours the hero develops into a superman of sorts and, if the screenwriter has done his or her job, so does the audience. In turn, the hero is implicitly deputized by that audience to act in its stead, up to and including killing in self-defense.

In short, through identification with the protagonist, each member of the audience has been transformed from a somewhat self-absorbed avoider of conflict into a powerful, decisive, self-sufficient person, prepared to face all manner of lethal threats with what Neill calls "a keenly sharpened vigilance" and a greatly enlarged reservoir of personal resources. If everything works, at least for a little while the theater is filled with people who have given up who they once were, their relatively immature selves, and have altered their perceptual universe so as to master an elemental threat. In Neill's analysis of the genre, the Thriller film, like the catharsis of Greek drama, thus provides a distinctive form of collective psychotherapy.

The author would especially like to thank the following writers and copyright holders for permission to use examples from their scripts:

North by Northwest written by Ernest Lehman ©1959 Turner Entertainment Co. All Rights Reserved.

Shane written by A.B. Guthrie ©1952, ©Renewed 1980, Paramount Pictures. All Rights Reserved.

Into the Night written by Ron Koslow ©1985 Universal City Studios, Inc. All Rights Reserved.

3 Days of the Condor written by Lorenzo Semple Jr. and David Rayfiel from the James Grady novel ©1975 Paramount Pictures Corporation. All Rights Reserved.

The Man Who Knew Too Much written by John Michael Hayes from the Charles Bennett and D.B. Wyndham-Lewis story ©1955 Filwite Productions, Inc. Renewed 1983 Samuel Taylor & Patricia Hitchcock O'Connell, as Co-Trustees. All Rights Reserved.

Single White Female written by Don Roos from the John Lutz novel ©1992 Columbia Pictures Industries, Inc. All Rights Reserved.

Breakdown written by Jonathan Mostow and Sam Montgomery from the Jonathan Mostow story ©1997 by Paramount Pictures. All Rights Reserved.

Enemy of the State written by David Marconi ©Touchstone Pictures

Marathon Man written by William Goldman ©1976 Gelderse Maatschappij N.V. All Rights Reserved.

Executive Decision written by Jim Thomas & John Thomas ©1996, Warner Bros.

NOT YOUR FATHER'S SCREENWRITING BOOK

The Thriller screenwriter's primary objective is to create fear in the audience — not the dazed fear of a Horror film, or even the anxious trepidation of self-discovery that occurs in the Personal Quest genre, but a sensation of edgy vigilance that should niggle the audience as they exit the theater to the outside world. There should be an extra glance over the shoulder now and then, a shiver of peripheral instinct that something is not quite known. The *reality* of the everyday world has become disjointed.

Reality, of course, is one of those words in English whose meaning can be pieced together only through the context in which it is used, and so *Writing the Thriller Film* explores several perspectives on reality that swirl together in the genre to create fear in the audience.

There is, first of all, the external, real-world reality that makes up our daily experience. This is the reality of traffic, bills, jobs — the customary stuff of life. It is this reality that the audience expects to be relieved of for a brief time when they enter a movie theater, all the while recognizing that they can never be completely removed from their deep-rooted experience of *real* life.

The second reality is the fictional reality of the screenwriter's story. It is a false reality, a fictitious delusion created in order to tell only one particular story. Yet the cosmos of the screenwriter's pretend-world must be perceived as real.

These two realities converge in a third: the perceptions that are held by the main character of a Thriller. It is in the mind of the protagonist that the skillful writer creates the alchemy that transforms the audience's interpretation of the real-world outside the theater into a sense of foreboding that hangs with them long after the movie is finished.

In order to investigate the vortex of realities that constitute the Thriller film, this book is organized somewhat differently than the two previous works, *Screenwriting 101: The Essential Craft Of Feature Film Writing* and *Writing the Action-Adventure Film: The Moment of Truth*. There are a good many fundamentals of solid screenplay structure and character development and other more or less procedural aspects of screenwriting that have not been hammered out in these pages because they are thoroughly covered in the previous two works. Instead, this book concentrates on the concealed bulwarks. Inside a great medieval cathedral, one should marvel at the captive heavens soaring above. Inside the Thriller story, the reader should never be aware of the flying buttresses that hold the walls in place. *Writing the Thriller Film*, therefore, concentrates on the Cosmos of Credibility, those not-so-obvious elements of screenwriting that contribute the essential *meaning* to a script. To do so, the book traces the thematic commonalities that actually define the genre, and offers corroboration from a number of screenplays, including classics such as *North by Northwest*, *Marathon Man*, and *3 Days of the Condor* — where the fundamental elements are relatively trouble-free to extract from the overall fabric of the script.

A WORD ABOUT WORDS

Although every effort has been made to retain the original screenwriters' style in the cited examples, in some instances a moderate amount of editing has been necessary in order to condense a scene for space, or to help focus an out-of-context selection.

Screenwriting style is highly idiosyncratic, so none of these examples should be regarded as models for imitation. What's more, the actual fashion of how words are set down on the page has changed radically over the years. An example:

```
EXT.   UNITED NATIONS HEADQUARTERS — DAY

As seen from the north, a LONG HIGH ANGLE
SHOT showing the General Assembly building in
the foreground, the 39-story marble and glass
Secretariat building beyond it, and in the
background, the East River and the Brooklyn
skyline.  At the extreme right, a taxi-cab is
seen pulling up at the curb near the main
entrance to the General Assembly building.
```

This shot description from *North by Northwest*, written by Ernest Lehman, is in a style that would never appear in a screenplay written today. The amount of detail, not to mention the directorial indications, are simply not necessary. The now-dated style notwithstanding, Lehman's *North by Northwest* is regarded as one of the most perfectly structured scripts ever written.

IT COULD HAPPEN TO ME

Thrillers should be disturbing. They should rupture your accepted reality. Put you on guard. Make you *aware*. That is the disquieting objective of this book as well.

CHAPTER 1

WHO MAKES THIS STUFF UP?

If you've ever fought back a mini-psychotic break while scrambling through the warehouse of videos at your local rental outlet in search of a particular movie, or even tried to locate a film by category in the massive Internet Movie Database (www.imdb.com), you know how aggravating a lack of standard organization for film genres can be. The film *Basic Instinct*, for example, might be cataloged as Mystery, Crime, Thriller, Horror, or even Action, depending on who assessed the movie for classification. And therein lies the confusion. Blockbuster, Hollywood Video, and all the other retail outlets are in the business of renting and selling movies, not the critical analysis of cinema. In order to create anything like an accurate register, they would have to have a specially trained staff look for particular elements in every film in their inventory and then tag those films accordingly. Of course, even if commercial outlets were willing to invest the resources necessary to develop a system, the customers themselves would have to be educated in how to use such a sophisticated scheme in order to make the system work.

In the larger commercial sense, then, the question of *meaning* for labels such as Action-Adventure, Thriller, Horror, etc. is virtually impossible to pin down without considering the context in which they are used. It probably is not important that the average audience member identify a particular film with an accurate label. What is important is that the audience is genuinely moved to laugh or cry or scream in outrage or shudder in terror because they have been deeply affected by a well-crafted story. But because the genre forms are so widely misconstrued within the movie industry itself, not the least by studio publicity departments, the defining terms have become truly vacuous expressions, loose lingo that each person interprets from an idiosyncratic point of reference. "Hey, we're doing this hard action character relationship story about an adventure into psychological terror, you know." With fuzzy thought and linguistic vagueness as the starting point, it's little wonder that our contemporary movie screens are filled with jangled narratives.

ALL ABOUT US!

– Title of NBC Television Saturday morning program

If the real significance of film genres is fuddled, it is because, in the pell-mell hustle to make a buck, movies and their sycophant medium television offer us ever more sparkly enticements with no anchor of substance, until the audience truly has no notion of what kind of movie it is watching. Even filmmakers themselves have come to embrace a standard of popular entertainment governed only by *Gresham's Law of Bamboozlement*[1], where increasingly incoherent narratives apply an electric prod to over-stimulated nerves. Instead of drama's confrontation with the terror of personal vulnerability, today's audience is propitiated with ersatz jeopardy spiked by razzle-dazzle pretense. Soon enough, the anesthetized spectators need ramped-up voltages to goose their sizzled synapses, until getting zapped is all that matters. "Okay, let's, uh, do it again. Whatever."

---

[1] "Bad money drives out good." An economic principle that cheap, inflated currency soon destroys the value of money backed by reserves, formulated by Sir Thomas Gresham (1519-1579), founder of the London Stock Exchange.

Yet, the audience can hardly be held entirely accountable for their cravings. From the time we first gawked at a television set, our egos have been pumped up, our insecurities have been soothed, our images flattered, and wishes we did not even know about have been gratified. Popular culture itself has become a soporific drone without which we have no resistance to the harsh clanging of human frailty.

Neither are the movies themselves completely deserving of blame. In spite of the yoke of accountability that some social critics would clamp on Hollywood films, movies are neither the architects nor the destroyers of culture. They are entertainment, pure and simple. Hollywood has always been an industry of exploitation rather than invention. Movies play catch-up with their surroundings like echoes refracted off the public psyche. Of course, the very best films are not merely repositories of societal artifact, but somehow encapsulate a truth that ricochets in our collective consciousness. The worst, lacking vision of authorship and courage of construction, are flat rebounds, already in cultural arrears, and far too faint to deliver more than a curious distraction for the audience.

On the other hand, simply because movies are an entertainment medium, and because audiences seek out pleasure, does not negate film's larger role in society. Movies should be capable of transcending the sheer cruddiness that so often affronts us. But even if the medium were never to exceed the limits of mass taste, there is no reason why films cannot be richer, less pandering, and more fully expressive through the work of conscientious authors.

Screenwriters are the lyricists of our cultural anthem. As such, we must captivate not with ferocious clamor, but by the masterful spinning of yarns. The scribbler's art is to make sense out of tribulations, vilify wickedness, extol gifts of character, delight in the foibles of humankind — and lie like there's no tomorrow.

CHAPTER 2

THE EXPECTATIONS OF GENRE

Ironically, a good storyteller uses linguistic sleight-of-hand to create a bond of trust with the audience. It is a credibility that depends on keeping the fabrications of fiction contained just inside the boundaries of a particular genre: a narrative scheme, distinctive characters, and a singular context. These conventions allow the audience to find a secure place from which to enjoy a voyage into the unfamiliar territory of the writer's story.

It is only comparatively recently, however, that the concept of motion picture *genre* has come to signify different types of stories instead of being a term for an entire class of "B" movies. Not too long ago, a "genre picture" simply meant a cheaply made screen filler, frequently of the Horror or Detective variety, and at the time, knowing that you were going to see a "Horror" movie was enough to set up certain expectations of what you would get. More and more, however, movies began to loan elements from one genre to another, and the rules of audience expectation turned topsy-turvy. At first, these portmanteau movies were just another form of theatrical exploitation. A "teen" picture might be mixed with "Horror" film elements in order to exploit both potential audiences. But as society owned up to its growing complexities, so did movies. Eventually, a movie like *Rebel Without a Cause*, for instance, took the surface elements of girls in tight sweaters and boys with hot-rods from the innocuous mush of teen movies, and incorporated them into a story that drew its power from the lacerated emotions of stage drama.

The contours of story soon became blurred. If it was a good idea to have a car chase in an action picture, why not put one into a story of psychological breakdown? The audience loves having the bad guy impaled on a church steeple. Let's do that in a comedy story. Sex is always good, so we'll shoehorn lots of that into the prison escape plot, even if we have to use a crowbar.

Naturally, there is no shortage of intellectual hypotheses concerning genres, but nearly all of these erudite approaches fall into one of two categories: film theory and social philosophy.

In academe, discussions of film genre frequently tend to rely on the fanciful notion that cinema is a *fait accompli* in much the same way as literature. In fact, courses in genre film are often cross-listed in English as well as Cinema departments. In general, these critical theory courses catalog genres only loosely by subject matter such as Western movies, Gangster films, Musicals, etc., or by immediately apparent surface-level characteristics such as action or humor. At times, whole courses are devoted to the false-genre cubbyholes of the instructor's favorite actor or director.

Meanwhile, the intellectual press has broadened the study of film theory into the realm of social commentary. One of the most influential analysts among the pop culture mavens prior to Marshall McLuhan[2], Robert Warshow[3] evaluated the Westerns and Gangster "genres" as *societal dramas*, for example. In the late 1960s, a new field of mass-culture analysis called *semiotics* became a major approach to the study of popular media as indicators of public values. An offshoot of linguistics, semiotics "aims to take in any system of signs, whatever their substance and limits, images,

---

[2] Marshall McLuhan, *Understanding Media: The Extensions of Man*, (McGraw-Hill, 1964).

[3] Robert Warshow, *The Immediate Experience: Movies, Comics, Theatre and Other Aspects of Popular Culture*, (Simon & Schuster, 1970).

gestures, musical sounds, objects, and the complex associations of all of these, which form the content of ritual, convention or public entertainment...."[4]

Film genres have been amply studied from one point of view or another. However, all of the theorizing on genre by scholars and social critics, while interesting in its own right, has accomplished very little to categorize the principles of film types in a systematic way that is useful to *screenwriters*. The wide variations in what are considered genres, not to mention the sub-classifications, socio-cultural nitpicking, and simple individual bias are just so much bookish balderdash when you're trying to make a script work.

Nonetheless, writers, directors, and studio executives are not relieved from the necessity to produce pictures that stay within breed, for it is only by studying the conventions of form that the creative members of the movie team can work out a truly *audience-focused* point-of-view, and the executive members can communicate well-informed critical assessments.

DO, OR DO NOT. THERE IS NO TRY.

– YODA

Screenwriting may be the only profession on earth outside of preaching where the totally untutored who have no groundwork or know-how believe that success will come through inspiration alone. Excellent screenwriting, though, is not an upchucking of emotional fragments, regardless of how heartfelt the urge may be. Giving birth to words on paper still involves labor. Over thousands of pages, the writer acquires an *earned instinct*, a tuned

---

[4] Roland Barthes, *Elements of Semiology*, (Jonathan Cape, 1967).

awareness to the nuances of what makes a good story, the voices of characters, and the constant vigilance to make certain the reader is located at the right place.

Likewise, the audience has developed an innate anticipation for the context elements it expects a particular genre to satisfy. Nevertheless, they must be convinced to give up their cautious reserve and defer reliance on everyday reality in favor of the dramatic movie world. To sell them on that world, the writer promises to tell the story within limits, that is, to establish a substitute reality that the audience can easily accept for the time being. This **Cosmos of Credibility** is composed of a **Narrative Trajectory**, a **Bounded World**, the **Timescape**, and a **Character Ethos** that are consistent within a given genre.

If the consistency is broken, if the Cosmos of Credibility is ruptured, the audience loses not only its belief in the special reality of the movie, but its trust in the storyteller as well. To say that there are rules, however, does not mean that movie genres are rigidly bound in their expressive elements. Some genres share certain characteristics, or the potential to have those characteristics, with others. The ubiquitous car chase, for instance, might occur in any genre, although certainly it is more fitting in Action-Adventure, Thriller, Detective, or perhaps even the Horror genres than it is in the less physically active forms. Nevertheless, the concept of a chase is not restricted to any particular type of film.

THE GENRE CONTINUUM

Obviously, movies' facility to scrounge actions from one genre to another is a reason why types of films are difficult to classify. So, in order to find a useful system for screenwriters, there must be an arrangement that relies on something other than interchangeable parts. Otherwise, we might as well talk about the "car chase" film genre, or even "pig movies," of which there has been a surprising number. Sometimes a form that might appear to be a genre at face value, such as science fiction, in fact is only a conglomeration of parts that have very little in common with each other. *Star Wars*, *Alien*, *Aliens*, *The Matrix*, and even *The Sixth Sense* could all be considered science fiction, although they are quite obviously very different films in virtually all respects. Pretty soon, then, arrangements into the various hodgepodges of arbitrary categorizations reveal themselves to be a waste of time for anyone except the academic and social theorists.

Instead, the **Genre Continuum**, an analytical concept that was introduced in *Screenwriting 101: The Essential Craft Of Feature Film Writing*, represents ten genres whose distinctions are drawn from deep-seated divergences in plot, character motivation, and restrictions of time and place — the supporting structure of movies rather than the immediately observable surface characteristics. Naturally, any given genre may share a few personality traits with its nearby neighbors, or even with distant relatives, and the continuum may not be end-to-end fail-safe, but it is a very useful tool to guide writers and producers in establishing audience trust.

THE FUNDAMENTALS OF GENRE

✓ **PRIVATE ANGUISH** — many European films, early Ingmar Bergman films

❑ **Narrative Trajectory** — These stories tend to be about characters' self-revelation through the expiation of guilt or imagined guilt. There is very little narrative plot because the events are contained largely inside the character. The Narrative Trajectory, then, is as unfixed as the main character, having no clear end point that the audience can foresee.

❑ **Bounded World** — Because the stories are essentially static, they occur in enclosed, usually small places that physically entrap the main character in internal anguish.

❑ **Timescape** — The timeline is a fairly short but intense climax of a lifetime of distress.

❑ **Character Ethos** — The characters are existential, tormented by their own self-doubts.

✓ **PIVOTAL CONFLICT** — *Ordinary People,*
Terms of Endearment, Tender Mercies, Steel
Magnolias, Marvin's Room, In The Bedroom

❑ **Narrative Trajectory** — Generally, estranged
family members are forced into interpersonal
conflict at an emotionally sensitive event such as
a funeral, which sets the scene for reviving and
resolving old wounds.

❑ **Bounded World** — The action occurs in a box-
like, inescapable setting that forces the characters
to deal with their quarrels. These films of pivotal
conflict in characters' lives are often made from
material that originally appeared as stage dramas
occurring in one room or primarily one room.

❑ **Timescape** – The pivotal conflict usually occurs
over a short period of time such as a weekend or
a couple of days because the sheer intensity of
the emotions demands that the characters resolve
their discord relatively quickly.

❑ **Character Ethos** – These characters are perhaps
the most frail, vulnerable, dimensional, and
thoroughly *human* in movies because their
conflicts are the most like those experienced by
ordinary audience members.

✓ **COMEDIC DRAMA** — *Modern Times, The General, Bringing Up Baby, La Cage Aux Folles, Tootsie, As Good As It Gets, What Women Want*

❑ **Narrative Trajectory** — Comic Dramas are about adults acting like children. There is a basic misunderstanding, a leap to the wrong conclusion that is never dealt with rationally. The characters are intimidated by a fascinating and bewildering world they are unprepared to deal with.

❑ **Bounded World** — The comedy world is a giant banana peel, intimidating, exaggerated, and filled with slick things and precarious people.

❑ **Timescape** — Because of the exaggeration of the story, the audience recognizes that the unreality of comedy cannot exist forever, so time is intense, frenetic, and short.

❑ **Character Ethos** — Comedy characters are the most nihilistic of cinema. They can get away with virtually anything within the riotous world defined by the film, but are generally still held accountable by the audience for the morality of their actions.

✓ **FAIRY TALE** — *Pretty Woman, The Piano, Sense and Sensibility, Good Will Hunting, Titanic, Moulin Rouge!*

❑ **Narrative Trajectory** — Fairy Tale characters must release themselves from the emotional bondage that they are subjected to by more dominant characters, who are customarily family members.

❑ **Bounded World** — The physical world is as restrictive as the main character's emotional or spiritual world, e.g., a sinking ship, a rural hamlet, or a primitive island.

❑ **Timescape** — Time is most often controlled by the characters themselves as they choose whether or not to act on their own behalf.

❑ **Character Ethos** — Characters are emblematic rather than dimensional, and very sharply defined as good or bad.

✓ **PERSONAL QUEST** — *Quiz Show, Chariots of Fire, Dead Man Walking, The Shawshank Redemption, Cast Away, A Beautiful Mind*

❑ **Narrative Trajectory** — The main character is compelled to define and achieve a personal quality, such as integrity or honesty, because of a moral crisis that demands immediate action.

❑ **Bounded World** — The Personal Quest often occurs in a physically constrained situation such as a prison or a hospital, or a position that is outside of the main character's control, such as the military, a sports team, or a corporation.

❑ **Timescape** — It may take weeks or months for the main character to come to grips with the Personal Quest, although an extreme event will always loom as the consummate trial for the main character's integrity.

❑ **Character Ethos** — These characters struggle with the conflict between an equivocal virtue versus moral certitude to determine the value of integrity.

✓ **DETECTIVE** — *Chinatown, The Maltese Falcon, The Usual Suspects, Se7en, The Silence of the Lambs*

❑ **Narrative Trajectory** — On the backside of civilization, the detective tries to restore equilibrium to a society that has developed a malignant infection.

❑ **Bounded World** — The detective, with or without a badge, patrols a decaying world of shadows and urban detritus.

❑ **Timescape** — Time is blurred, neither day nor night, and as vaporously shrouded as an intoxicated stupor.

❑ **Character Ethos** — The detective is a thinker, a character of wits rather than physical strength, who seeks the truth on the shady side of the street.

✓ **HORROR** — *Frankenstein, Dracula, Friday the 13th, Halloween, Poltergeist, Invasion of the Body Snatchers*

❏ **Narrative Trajectory** — A supernatural monster has absolute power over its human victims, who must discover its secret vulnerability in order to survive.

❏ **Bounded World** — Terror exists in a distorted world riddled with secret passageways and unknown recesses, isolated from any outside salvation.

❏ **Timescape** — Because isolation is essential, the intense action occurs over a very short time, usually twenty-four hours or less.

❏ **Character Ethos** — The characters are *everyman*, extremely vulnerable yet resourceful, representing the best of the human spirit in battle against the evil of an inhuman fiend.

✓ **THRILLER** — *3 Days of the Condor, North by Northwest, Alien, Single White Female, Breakdown*

❏ **Narrative Trajectory** — The audience experiences an intense identification with the main character's willingness to stay alive.

❏ **Bounded World** — The main character is isolated from help by physical circumstance and psychologically isolated by betrayal.

❏ **Timescape** — The extreme isolation from outside help enforces a short, but intense timeline as the main character's fears overtake rational perception.

❏ **Character Ethos** — A comparatively uninvolved character is drawn into an increasingly larger menace, and discovers that the only way to remain alive is through self-reliance, by exposing the malevolent evil before it can assault the larger community.

✓ **ACTION-ADVENTURE** — all Westerns, War Movies, Cops & Robbers films, *Braveheart, Star Wars, The Guns Of Navarone, Con Air, Saving Private Ryan, Gladiator*

❑ **Narrative Trajectory** —The main character knowingly undertakes an impossible mission to save a society from a state of siege, and willingly faces death to defend a personal code of honor that the society shares as a value.

❑ **Bounded World** — The surroundings are open, available for action, and beyond everyday experience.

❑ **Timescape** — Often a sense of weeks, months, or even years during which a state of siege builds unbearable tension that must be broken by decisive action.

❑ **Character Ethos** — Characters who are willing to die for an idea, code, society, or value, battle equally motivated antagonists who are *morally different* in a showdown moment of truth.

✓ **METAPHYSICAL DEFIANCE** — *Crimes and Misdemeanors, Amadeus*

❑ **Narrative Trajectory** — The main character risks an immortal soul by challenging the authority of a self-indulgent Almighty.

❑ **Bounded World** — A sophisticated setting, usually surrounded by the trappings of power and position, where characters have achieved the status of God on earth.

❑ **Timescape** — The main character only slowly comes to recognize that the struggle is against God.

❑ **Character Ethos** — Characters are intelligent, highly successful, but morally untested, and battle to exert their self-concept over that of an irrational, unjust God.

In addition to providing ways to classify films, the Genre Continuum (see page 23) also ranks the genres in a specific sequence from left to right, starting with films of Private Anguish where characters are trapped within themselves, and ending with those rare films of Metaphysical Defiance, where mankind directly challenges an infinite God. The order of the progression is determined by how the main character acts to resolve the core challenge of the film story, how that action changes the society contained within the context of the movie, and what effect that change has on the members of the movie audience.

Reading from left to right, each genre has an expanding influence on the society that contains its story in direct proportion to the degree of lethal threat that the main character suffers. That is, the greater the risk there is in the story that the main character will die, the more there is at stake not only for that character but for the surrounding characters, up to and including an entire cultural body or way of life. If Luke Skywalker doesn't destroy the Death Star, not only will he die, but the entire rebel society will likely be destroyed. On the other hand, if Julia Roberts does not get married (pick a movie), it is doubtful that the nation will fall into the clutches of an evil overlord.

The first section of the Genre Continuum contains films in the Private Anguish, Pivotal Conflict, Comedic Drama, Fairy Tale, and Personal Quest genres, all of which share a fundamental goal that the main character seeks to make life more complete, to live a richer existence in some fashion. For example, one of the most popular film genres is the Fairy Tale. In fact, the most commercially successful film of all time, *Titanic*, owes its phenomenal achievement in part to the fact that the *this-happens* and because of it *that-happens* plot is undemanding. All of the characters are clearly good or bad. In spite of the momentous tragic event which constitutes the context for *Titanic*, the doomed love affair of a boy and girl is universally identifiable, and our identification with this story gives the ill-fated love affairs of our own past a kind of majesty that makes *sense*. This elegant simplicity, along with other elements, is shared by *Pretty Woman*, *Good Will Hunting*, *Moulin Rouge!*, and dozens of other successful films that, for the purposes of genre classification, are Fairy Tales.

These simple stories have certain structure, character, and context elements that are nearly identical. However, there may be a film about two people in love on a doomed ship — without all of the additional Fairy Tale elements — that would not fall into the Fairy Tale genre. *The African Queen*, for instance, is about two people on a doomed boat who fall in love, but the film is decidedly an Action-Adventure story rather than of a Fairy Tale[5].

The defining difference is what influences the actions of the lovers, Jack and Rose in *Titanic*, have on their story, their immediate society, and the society of the audience. Of course they influence Rose's fiancé and her mother, but these people are about to be greatly overwhelmed by events outside Rose's power. The remaining fact is that the love affair between Jack and Rose does not change the surrounding society one bit. Nothing they do has any effect whatsoever on the social order, world affairs, or who does what to whom in any larger sphere.

So, although the emotion of the story can, and obviously does have an enormously potent impact on the audience, that audience is not bonded to any societal change caused by the actions of the main characters. Furthermore, the risks that the main characters take are *comparatively* small. The principal goal for the two lovers in *Titanic* is to improve their individual lives, that is, to enlarge their joy and become fully alive. The risks these characters take, although they may be emotionally terrifying, do not have *lethal* consequences. Failure to achieve the goal of happily-ever-after

---

[5] For a more complete discussion of *The African Queen*, see *Writing the Action-Adventure Film* (ISBN 0-941188-39-6).

21

may lead to despondency, but nobody *expects* to risk death in the process. In *Titanic*, although Jack does indeed die, he does not anticipate that possibility anymore than the others on the ship, and, in fact, his death is not actually compelled by the plot.

The distinctive characters and themes that play out in these various genres are the compositional nuts and bolts that create an atmosphere of trust for the audience. If these components are in place, the audience unconsciously knows that the story they are watching will, in the end, be worth the investment of their time. This does not mean, of course, that every story in a particular genre is identical, much less that is it predictable, but simply that after some ten thousand years of storytelling, we have a pretty good idea of what motivates an audience.

The audience immediately becomes suspicious, though, when the writer leaves the storyline vulnerable to the illicit migration of unsuitable elements from one movie genre to another. The film *Copycat*, for instance, is hypothetically a Thriller. A psychiatrist played by Sigourney Weaver studies serial killers, but she suffers from agoraphobia and is terrified to set foot outside her own apartment. One of her subjects begins a campaign of terror against her via her computer. As a Thriller this set-up has good possibilities. The main character is in jeopardy, isolated, and must overcome her own internal fears if she chooses to save her life. It is not unlike the very successful stage play and subsequent movie *Wait Until Dark*, in which Audrey Hepburn plays a blind woman trapped inside her apartment by killers. However, rather than restricting itself to the tight confines of a Thriller, *Copycat* destroys

METAPHYSICAL DEFIANCE
THE GENRE CONTINUUM

⇧ INCREASING PERSONAL JEOPARDY EQUALS ⇧ INCREASING SOCIETAL CONSEQUENCE

WILLINGNESS TO BECOME FULLY ALIVE					WILLINGNESS TO LIVE			WILLINGNESS TO DIE	
PRIVATE ANGUISH	PIVOTAL CONFLICT	COMEDIC DRAMA	FAIRY TALE	PERSONAL QUEST	DETECTIVE	HORROR	THRILLER	ACTION-ADVENTURE	METAPHYSICAL DEFIANCE
Many European films; early Ingmar Bergman films	Ordinary People, Terms of Endearment, Tender Mercies, Marvin's Room, In the Bedroom, etc.	Modern Times, The General, Bringing Up Baby, Tootsie, As Good As It Gets, What Women Want, etc.	Pretty Woman, The Piano, Good Will Hunting, Titanic, Moulin Rouge!, etc.	Dead Man Walking, Quiz Show, The Shawshank Redemption, Cast Away, A Beautiful Mind, etc.	Se7en, The Maltese Falcon, Chinatown, The Usual Suspects, The Silence of the Lambs, etc.	Poltergeist, Frankenstein, Dracula, Friday the 13th, Halloween, etc.	North by Northwest, 3 Days of the Condor, Alien, Breakdown, etc.	Braveheart, Gladiator, Star Wars, Guns of Navarone, Saving Private Ryan, etc.	Crimes and Misdemeanors, Amadeus, etc.

the contract of trust with the audience by bringing in an outside rescuer, a tough cop played by Holly Hunter, to save Sigourney Weaver. The intervention of Hunter's inappropriate cop leaves the audience confused about what kind of movie they're supposed to be watching, Thriller or Action-Adventure?

The middle section of the Genre Continuum includes Detective, Horror, and Thriller. Although all of these genres may share some common elements with each other, they are distinct forms involving different characters who seek different goals. What they have in common is a choice that ultimately faces the main character about the willingness to stay alive.

Thriller stories are about ordinary people who are unprepared for the life-threatening situation that envelops them. When the chips are down, driven to exhaustion and alone with no help available, will the main character find the strength required to remain biologically functional?

CHAPTER 3

THE COSMOS OF CREDIBILITY

Of popular film genres, i.e., those that studios are most likely to finance because the largest audience buys tickets to see them, the Thriller is by far the most difficult screenplay to write. Whereas an Action-Adventure or the various styles of Comedy allow for a good deal of latitude in the audience's willing suspension of disbelief, the success of a Thriller depends almost entirely on the filmmakers' ability to confidently assure the audience that they are watching near-documentary authenticity, while simultaneously hoodwinking them into giving up their dependence on the real world altogether.

It may seem odd that we go to the movies hoping to be entertained by an illusion, and yet remain tightly bound to our familiar interpretations of life. As any screenwriter knows, the audience simply does not give in to the movie fantasy as easily as it may appear to observers outside of the industry. A movie has to be *sold*, that is, the audience must be coaxed or bullied or surprised into a wholehearted participation in the artificial world on the movie screen. In this respect, films are no different from other narrative forms that aim to create images in the mind. Listeners quite willingly hitch a ride on the imaginary, hypnotic journeys of poets, storytellers, and singers. The difference is that the experience of literature, dance, and even music is relatively muted compared to cinema. It is one thing to suspend disbelief during a live theatre presentation where a constant peripheral awareness extends beyond the proscenium to tinkle the chimes of reality, and quite another to be seduced by the siren song of a movie that is literally larger than life. But the mantra of film also has a devious refrain that invites us to leave our common sense at the door, and that is an abandonment that our very human nature resists.

THE VIRTUAL PRESENT

Many philosophers and film theorists have attempted to draw paradigms for a movie aesthetic that both embraces us and keeps us at arm's length, including Susanne Langer, who popularized the now famous pronouncement that, "Cinema is like dream."

> ...I do not mean that it copies dream, or puts one into a daydream... [Cinema] creates a virtual present, an order of direct apparition. That is the mode of dream... the dreamer is always at the center of it. Places shift, persons act and speak, or change or fade – facts emerge, situations grow, objects come into view with strange importance, ordinary things infinitely valuable or horrible, and they may be superseded by others that are related to them essentially by feeling, not by natural proximity. But the dreamer is always "there," his relation is, so to speak, equidistant from all events. Things may occur around him or unroll before his eyes; he may act or want to act, or suffer or contemplate; but the immediacy of everything in a dream is the same for him. This aesthetic peculiarity... creates a virtual present[6].

---

[6] Susanne Langer, *Feeling and Form*, (Charles Scribner's Sons, 1953).

The immediacy of the virtual present creates, in effect, a *hyper-reality* for the audience. The images and sounds on the screen are more intense than everyday life itself. And yet, the audience's internal gyroscope is still oriented to the up and down and right and left of the tangible world, which creates a dilemma for the screenwriter. A subtle balance must be maintained between keeping the audience convinced that the story occurs to people "just like us," while simultaneously knocking the props out from under authenticity so that those everyday characters can be swept up credibly into a larger-than-life story.

... WHEN YOU HAVE EXCLUDED THE IMPOSSIBLE, WHATEVER REMAINS, HOWEVER IMPROBABLE, MUST BE THE TRUTH.

– Sherlock Holmes, *The Adventure of the Beryl Coronet*
by Sir Arthur Conan Doyle

When an audience enters the theater willing to suspend their disbelief, they know that what they are about to see is not real. In fact, they came to the movie precisely because they want to experience something that makes more sense than the outside world. So, although the Thriller plot is contrived, it must look as if it grows naturally from the "real" circumstances of the story. Moreover, an audience expects the world of the movie to be not only sharper and more comprehensible than the everyday world they live in, but to provide them with a paradigm for the way the real world could be.

Yet, precisely because the audience knows the general patterns and procedures of daily life, they are constantly on the lookout for any violation. Thriller characters must consistently behave in ways that ordinary people believe they, themselves, would react in the

27

same circumstances if pushed to similar extremes. If the audience ever has reason to ask the characters, "Why don't you just...," then the illusion of reality is broken. They know, for instance, that in the real world the washed-out bridge that has isolated the characters would be replaced after a reasonably short period of time, so there are implicit limits on how much liberty the story can assume. The screenwriter must preclude rational analysis from interfering with the peculiar logic of the movie by establishing the rules by which the audience views the reality of the film, that is, the Cosmos of Credibility within which the story is played out.

THE COSMOS OF CREDIBILITY

NARRATIVE TRAJECTORY is the overarching structure that establishes a sense of completeness for the story.

BOUNDED WORLD is the environment and objects that impact the physical actions and psychological responses of the characters.

TIMESCAPE is the chronological and psychological time frame in which the story takes place.

CHARACTER ETHOS is the moral code that influences characters' dramatic choices.

Some rules have already been established by default. In deciding to tell a particular story, the screenwriter is already locked into the inherent boundaries of time and place. A Thriller film certainly is not the same as a Musical Comedy, for example. Less obviously, a Thriller film does not exist in the same Cosmos of Credibility as a Horror film, Action-Adventure film, or any other genre. Of course, film is a collaborative medium, so the final responsibility for a film's contextual world is difficult to pin down. Like the allegory of the blind men describing the elephant, the identification of the most significant element of credibility depends on whose job it is to create that component. It is absolutely certain, however, that if the screenwriter does not conscientiously lay out the organic boundaries of time, space, and character on the page, the conglomeration of the filmmaking group will surely construct a camel instead of an elephant.

Scribble Exercise:

DETECTIVE	THRILLER	ACTION-ADVENTURE

Classify the following films according to the genre you believe they represent:

Aliens	*Shoot to Kill*
Broken Arrow	*Rear Window*
Coma	*Charade*
Air Force One	*Brainstorm*
Rear Window	*Forbidden Planet*
The Silence of the Lambs	*Se7en*
Cape Fear	*Fatal Attraction*
Double Indemnity	*Klute*
Jagged Edge	*No Way Out*
Basic Instinct	*Reversal of Fortune*
Andromeda Strain	*The Perfect Storm*

CHAPTER 4

NARRATIVE TRAJECTORY

Good screenwriting is much more than a *hot-scripts-in-five-cool-moves* recipe. It is the sense of overarching impact that's made on the audience by the totality of the screenplay's parts. Any given scene arising from one or more structural elements may, by itself, create a memorable impression on the audience. The graphic murder scene in Alfred Hitchcock's *Psycho* kept many women out of the bathroom shower for years. Likewise, the memory of Babe's (Dustin Hoffman) suffering at the hands of Szell (Lord Laurence Olivier) in *Marathon Man* can give you a bad case of the willies whenever a dentist says, "Open wide." But the effectiveness of a good Thriller film must be judged by the overall spirit that propels an audience from the opening scene through the unfolding story. Like the arched flight of an arrow, the audience's anticipation rises from the angle of release at the beginning, bending to the apex of complications, through the promise of final resolution that draws the story arrow to ground. It is the screenwriter's mastery of this encompassing *Narrative Trajectory*, the curve of the storyteller's arc, that the audience puts its trust in.

The brightest flares of interest on the arc, naturally, are the beginning where velocity is imparted, the middle where there is the maximum tension as the arrow strains against gravity, and the end, where the missile rockets down to bury its tip at a fixed point in the earth. These heightened interest points can also illustrate an *audience-focused* perspective on the job of telling a movie story.

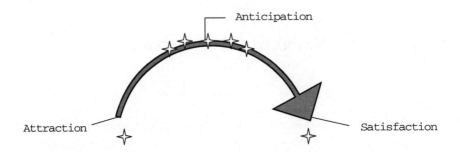

ATTRACTION

The audience is not so much interested in the character as in the character's predicament. In the beginning, the audience really wants to know what this story is *about*. How is the main character going to get out of the mess?

ANTICIPATION

The conflict between the main character and the antagonist increases so that the audience expects more and more interesting things to happen. Tension builds because the actions taken by the characters do *not* produce the expected results, and therefore the characters must make new decisions that will have new unknown results. It is the pressure of the unknown that creates suspense for the audience.

SATISFACTION

Because the antagonist is stronger than the main character, the hero must overcome internal fears as well as external obstacles. Only through character growth is the audience's anticipation satisfied by a complete story that, unlike the chaos of normal life, makes sense out of capricious reality.

A more linear way of looking at the Narrative Trajectory is recognizable as the long-established three-act structure.

AUDIENCE-FOCUSED SEQUENCE

BEGINNING	MIDDLE	END
ATTRACTION	ANTICIPATION	SATISFACTION
ACT I	ACT II	ACT III

Extravagant allegations for newly revealed methods of organization that claim to make the three-act structure obsolete have more to do with merchandising than with genuine structural analysis. All stories resolve themselves into three acts: a beginning, a middle, and an end. Regardless of how the segments are demarcated, or whether the middle is arranged before the beginning, as it is in *Casablanca*, for instance, a screenwriter organizes material so that the audience feels satisfied by the *gestalt* [7] that any good story *delivers* [8].

THE ASSAULT

Overall, the action of a Thriller surges from an initial Chase through a concluding State of Siege, exactly the opposite pathway from that followed by an Action-Adventure story. In an Action-Adventure story, the protagonist enters the drama at a point where all attempts at negotiation, tactics, and reconciliation have failed or are clearly of no use against an antagonist who is committed to

---

[7] gestalt: a configuration or pattern of elements so unified as a whole that it cannot be described merely as a sum of its parts

[8] For a more complete discussion of the three-act structure, please see *Screenwriting 101: The Essential Craft Of Feature Film Writing*, (ISBN 0-941188-72-8).

destruction or dominance. That is, the protagonist has no other options available to break the stalemate except physical force. The attack of physical force changes the dynamic of the story from a siege to a form of battle pursuit.

Thrillers, on the other hand, begin in a world that is seemingly free of conflict, at least as far as the main character is concerned. However, an assault on the main character's customary existence creates a natural reaction of fear and panic so that the protagonist's impulse is to run, which immediately sets up the Narrative Trajectory as a chase. Running away, though, does not lead to the expected freedom in a Thriller, but directly into the trap of isolation where the character is held captive by an overpowering force. That is, the chase lands the character smack in the middle of a State of Siege!

In *North by Northwest* Roger Thornhill (Cary Grant) is mistaken for a government agent by a group of spies who intend to kill him. But Thornhill has absolutely no idea why he is a target for death. No one believes the threat against him, so he takes the rational action that any normal person would take — *he runs away*. In *3 Days of the Condor*, Robert Redford's Joe Turner is a low-level CIA employee who returns to work after lunch to discover that everyone in his office has been brutally murdered. There's no time to wait around and figure things out. Turner *runs* to escape the same fate.

SELF-PRESERVATION

Now, in the real world, it may seem excessive to jettison the safety of family, friends, and the normal routine simply because of some disturbing coincidence or irregularity, no matter how intimidating it may seem at the moment. We can always go to the police, call an attorney, and rally our friends when our ordered existence is threatened.

But, what if those resources aren't there? What if none of our trusted channels of salvation will verify our experience, much less risk protecting us? What if you are the only person who believes in the threat, and you believe in it with the absolute conviction of stark fear! Now whatcha gonna do? Run! *Save your life.*

It is crucial that the screenwriter's aim in the Thriller Narrative Trajectory be riveted on the singular target of escape. Any self-indulgent side trips will throw the flight path off course so that the audience loses sight of what the story is supposed to be about, and will ensure that they cannot possibly be satisfied with the ending. This is particularly true if the Thriller genre is used as a forum for preachy socio-political harangues or snazzy visual effects that do not reinforce the constant *lethal threat* that dogs the main character.

For all of the well-crafted set-up of its ominous subject matter, *Enemy of the State* soon bogs down in razzmatazz stock footage editing and sidebar fluff which undermines the drive of the story, until the resolution becomes nothing more than comic buffoonery that is completely out of correlation with the film's sinister theme. In fact, even though the film begins as an excellent premise for a Thriller, it ignores the fundamental boundaries at so many points that it barely qualifies for the genre at all.

SUSPENSE

Naturally, in the beginning of a film neither the audience nor the main character knows exactly where the story is going, but the fact

WRITING THE THRILLER FILM / Hicks

that the character does not immediately know what is happening is not unique to the Thriller genre. The very nature of drama demands that characters must discover what is happening to them and make choices about how to respond to those demands. Thrillers, however, have a special conspiratorial relationship with the audience, often providing backstory information that the characters themselves do not possess. The information passed secretly to the audience may be about an insufficiency in the main character's life, or even about the antagonist's secret intentions. The storyteller's subterfuge infuses the entire Narrative Trajectory of a Thriller with *suspense*. At times, the audience may delight at the revelation that the antagonist's plan *cannot* work because of some unknown stratagem by the hero, then lose all hope when they realize, unlike the character, that the antagonist has the upper hand.

The intrigue of wits that puts the audience itself in the vicarious danger of a commonplace world turned ominous is the realm of acknowledged suspense master Alfred Hitchcock.

> There is a distinct difference between "suspense" and "surprise," and yet many pictures continually confuse the two. We are now having a very innocent little chat. Let us suppose that there is a bomb underneath this table between us. Nothing happens and then all of a sudden, "Boom!" There is an explosion. The public is surprised, but prior to this surprise, it has seen an absolutely ordinary scene, of no special consequence. Now let us take a suspense situation. The bomb is underneath the table and the public knows it. The public is aware that the bomb is going to explode at one o'clock and there is a clock in the decor. The public can see

that it is a quarter to one. In these conditions the same innocuous conversation becomes fascinating because the public is participating in the scene[9].

The kind of Thriller suspense that Hitchcock describes is not at all the same thing as the tension created by the genre's closest relatives, Action-Adventure, Detective, and Horror. While Action-Adventure films may deliberately withhold information from the characters or the audience, this narrative stinginess is rarely a motif that runs throughout the film — because Action-Adventure is about the action of identifying an objective and achieving it. The surprises along the way are obstacles that the hero must overcome, not fundamental changes in the direction of the story. In *Die Hard*, for instance, there is suspense created when the antagonist Hans Gruber (Alan Rickman) comes face-to-face with an apparently unsuspecting John McClane (Bruce Willis). Gruber pretends to be one of the hostages in the building and McClane even gives him a gun. For the audience, who know very well that Gruber is the antagonist, the scene is gripping. But because McClane presumably does not know the person he's dealing with, there is no simultaneous tension for the main character.

Detective genre films, especially of the *Who-Done-It?* form, frequently use the withholding of information from the audience as a kind of suspense. Detective mysteries such as *The Usual Suspects* and *The Sixth Sense* are intellectual puzzles that lure the audience into playing hide-and-seek along with the main detective character.

---

[9] Francois Truffaut, HITCHCOCK, (Simon and Schuster, 1966).

> "...The whodunit generates the kind of curiosity that is void of emotion, and emotion is an essential ingredient of suspense."[10]

Even the suspense of the Horror genre is quite different from that of the Thriller. Horror tends to use suspense as a set-up for shock, that is, a scene-by-scene prelude that establishes the conditions for sudden squeals and shrieks of audience reaction. Classically, Horror suspense is pumped up by sending an unsuspecting character down a passageway of some nature where the audience believes the story's monster lurks in wait. The character opens first one door and then another only to find that no monster leaps out, and the tension builds as the audience anticipates the inevitable confrontation. But when the character flings open the final door in the corridor to reveal nothing at all, the audience members — although mystified by their incorrect perceptions — relax their guard for an instant. That's long enough for the monster to leap from a hidden crevice to attack the hapless character, and the unsuspecting audience to reflexively jerk into emotional incontinence. It is this suspense/startle technique that is employed so well by Steven Spielberg in *Jaws* and John Carpenter in the original *Halloween*.

VELOCITY OF ACTION

In the beginning, all Thriller films contain two potential story lines: one Narrative Trajectory for the Protagonist, or main character, and a separate Narrative Trajectory for that main character's opposition, the Antagonist. Followed separately, each

---

[10] Ibid.

38

of these narratives would not be much more than episodic lists of events, and while the list for the antagonist would be more attention-grabbing because of the inherent threat it poses to the audience, without the intervention of the protagonist's narrative, it would contain no *drama* of conflict.

Imagine, for instance, an arbitrary protagonist: a college professor of chemistry who has a wife, two children, a dog, and a travel trailer for family vacations. Knowing nothing more that these spare details, it is possible to list the major events of the professor's life for the next twelve months, but it will be very difficult to find anything in that list that is worthy of a feature film story.

On the other hand, imagine an arbitrary antagonist: an enigmatic business executive whose respected environmental engineering company is actually a front for a series of strategically planned ecological catastrophes that will ultimately give him sole ownership control of all the electrical generating power west of the Rockies. Of course, it would be interesting to know how Mr. Antagonist intends to carry off this coup, what economic and political resources he has under his power, and exactly what the culminating event will be. Nevertheless, it is such a grandiose scheme that there is something not quite believable about it, so perfectly calculated that it is beyond human scope. There needs to be an element of surprise, a slip-up, the blunder of fate that brings this master conspiracy into affective focus.

And *that* is where the screenwriter creates a *story*. By some device, a contrivance, the ordinary hum-drum narrative of the chemistry professor intersects the megalomaniacal narrative of the executive, and the resultant clash fuses the two trajectories inseparably into one Thriller story that engages the emotions of the audience.

As soon as the protagonist interrupts the antagonist's story, the Thriller takes on the throbbing cadence of fear. The story suddenly plunges from the ordinary into the corridors of a labyrinth, where the main character desperately slams into closed doors and stone walls in search of the familiar reality that's been destroyed.

It is this disruption of the familiar that, in turn, creates an internal panic which clouds the character's perceptions and further drives the story into a maze of terror.

THE ANTAGONIST'S BROKEN NARRATIVE TRAJECTORY

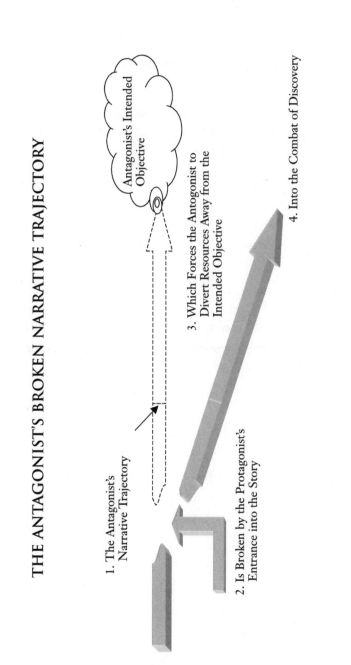

Antagonist's Intended Objective

1. The Antagonist's Narrative Trajectory

2. Is Broken by the Protagonist's Entrance into the Story

3. Which Forces the Antogonist to Divert Resources Away from the Intended Objective

4. Into the Combat of Discovery

41

Scribble Exercise:

❏ **What would the completed Narrative Trajectory of the antagonist be if the protagonist were never introduced into the following films?**

- *Air Force One*

- *Broken Arrow*

- *Enemy Of The State*

- *Jagged Edge*

❏ **Why is the protagonist in these films the *only* person who can interrupt the antagonist's Narrative Trajectory?**

CHAPTER 5

BOUNDED WORLD

The environment of any film story is unavoidably limited by the events that the writer chooses to include. Cutthroat pirates do not haunt the Seven Seas in Winnebago travel trailers. Each genre makes use of a certain *milieu* that is not only the container for the story, but functions as a manifestation of the drama that is going on *inside* the main character. The Personal Quest genre, for instance, includes such films as *The Shawshank Redemption, Quiz Show, Dead Man Walking*, and *A Beautiful Mind*, stories which take place in worlds that are highly constrained. The restrictions may be physical, such as a prison, or behavioral, such as a military or corporate organization, or both. In each case, though, there are strict boundaries within which the character is expected to conduct affairs, and outside of which the character may not stray.

An Action-Adventure, on the other hand, ordinarily occurs in a world that is behaviorally, if not always physically, freely available. The Westerns of John Ford, for example, use vast panoramas of untamed territory not merely as the wide-open spaces where physical action occurs, but also as expressions of the characters' wide-open forthrightness. Action-Adventure protagonists are bound only by their own sense of duty. Within that code, however, they are deputized to do whatever is necessary to stop the antagonist from destroying a threatened society. In *Shane*, the character of Shane himself is nearly always seen against a background of rugged mountains stretching into the infinite wilderness from which he came. Shane is a stranger. His physical world is unbound by the rules of society. His actions are those of personal freedom of choice rather than public expectations, and it is that freedom of choice that ultimately returns him to the wilderness.

                    SHANE
        I gotta be going on.

                    JOEY
        Why, Shane?

                    SHANE
        A man has to be what he is, Joey.
        You can't break the mold. I tried it
        and it didn't work for me.

                    JOEY
        We want you, Shane.

                    SHANE
        Joey, there's no living with a
        killing. There's no going back from
        one. Right or wrong, it's a brand.
        A brand that sticks. There's no
        going back.

The protagonists in all genres, then, are faced with the conflict between personal desire and public demands, lawful duty, family obligation, religious dedication, etc. It is a necessary part of drama that the main character must resolve inner needs in order to do battle with the external antagonist, so the reconciliation between truth and expectation is not, by itself, unique to any particular genre. It is the uniqueness of the boundaries of the physical and behavioral world within the Cosmos of Credibility for a particular drama that sets it apart from other genres.

THE INCREDIBLE BOUNDED BY THE RATIONAL

The world of the true Thriller film is an imaginative *What if...* that is bounded by real-world rules of physical expectations. *What if...* you were mistaken for an international spy, kidnapped, and found yourself running for your life? *What if...* your wife or your husband or your child was suddenly taken captive by ruthless criminals who are willing to kill unless they get what they want? *What if...*, as a hardworking corporate executive, salesman, university student, or librarian, you suddenly found yourself the key figure defending the safety of the President of the United States against cold-blooded terrorists? *What if...* a gorgeous woman jumped into your car and begged you to save her life?

The latter is exactly what happens to Jeff Goldblum as Ed Okin in *Into The Night*. Ed, a demoralized Los Angeles engineer whose wife is cheating on him and whose monotonous life has driven him to insomnia, decides to catch a midnight flight to Las Vegas and gamble away his worries. But, by sheer fate, this ordinary man enters the airport parking lot at the wrong time — or perhaps the right time — because from this instant on his life will never be dull again.

45

INT. PARKING STRUCTURE — GROUND LEVEL

As Ed waits for the elevator, another couple approaches — a striking couple. The WOMAN[11] is young and very pretty with long, sunstreaked hair and a sleek, sensuous body. She is elegantly dressed in a white Saint Laurent suit, a fur coat slung over her shoulder. The young MAN who escorts her looks vaguely Middle Eastern. He is casually but richly attired by Bijan. He carries her suitcase while his other hand guides her by the elbow. They walk quickly.

An awkward moment of silence as they all wait. The elevator doors open. Ed steps aside, allowing the Woman to enter. She starts in, but is subtly pulled back by her escort. He motions Ed to go ahead. Ed enters the elevator; the couple does not. As the doors close, Ed is too self-absorbed to be puzzled or insulted.

INT. PARKING STRUCTURE — THIRD LEVEL

Ed exits the elevator. The same menacing atmosphere, but he has other things on his mind — like, what now? Home? The possibilities don't seem so infinite... He climbs into his car.

---

[11] Michelle Pfeiffer

INT. ED'S CAR

He just sits in the car. "What is he doing
here?" Lost and defeated, he rests his
weary head on the steering wheel. He could
easily be mistaken for a tired man, or a
dead man — if anybody cared to notice.

THE ELEVATOR

Across the parking lot, the beautiful couple
step off the elevator. Suddenly TWO MEN
slip out from the shadows and attack them
from behind. Simultaneously, a white
Mercedes pulls up.

A violent struggle, the faces of the
attackers obscured by shadows.

The Woman, a hand clapped over her mouth, is
brutally shoved toward the waiting Mercedes.

Her escort attempts to pull a gun and is
ripped open by four silenced shots from an
automatic pistol. While the body, the fur
coat, and the suitcase are loaded in the
trunk of the Mercedes —

The Woman fights for her life. She manages
to land a solid kick to the kneecap of her
attacker and break away. As she runs,
cutting through a row of parked cars — one

47

terrible scream echoes through the parking structure. Her assailants momentarily freeze, then take off in pursuit.

INT. ED'S CAR

He is jolted alert. He looks around, hears RUNNING FEET, then sees:

ED'S POV

The Woman dashes madly across a parking lane, scrambling over and around parked cars, using them to gain distance from the Two Men who pursue her. Suddenly she seems to fall and disappear from view. The Two Men separate, so as to trap her. Is it a rape?... Is it a dream?

INT. ED'S CAR

His mind's racing — what to do? Get out? Get help? Get involved? Get killed? His hand on the ignition, he hesitates, realizing that if the engine doesn't catch, he'll be revealed. Maybe they already know he's there... Maybe the Men are police, and the Woman, a fugitive... or a lunatic.

THE WOMAN

crawling frantically on her belly, under a row of cars. The look of animal fear.

HER POV

The feet of one of her attackers, some distance away, but coming toward her.

ED'S CAR

He hits the ignition. The engine turns over and dies... He tries again — again no luck.

THE WOMAN

Still on her belly, she turns toward the sound of Ed's car. It's not far away — up ahead and maybe in the next row... she quickly checks back on her pursuers.

HER POV

The approaching feet have momentarily stopped. They turn slightly, as if also searching out the source of the car engine.

INT. ED'S CAR

He's swearing and praying. He tries again — squeezing every last volt from his battery. The engine of the old Toyota catches with an uncharacteristic roar. He throws it into gear.

THE WOMAN

She sees Ed's car start to move — backing
out of the adjacent row. She picks herself
up and runs for it, as he swings into the
parking lane. Her pursuers now spot her and
move quickly. They appear to be Middle
Eastern.

INT. ED'S CAR

Tooting his meager horn, hoping to summon
help, he sees the Two Men coming towards him
from opposite sides — but he doesn't see the
Woman. He starts to take off when she
appears on his blind side, banging on the
passenger window, trying to get in.

For a split second, their eyes meet. Her
desperation nearly melts the glass. Slowing
down, Ed unlocks the door. She leaps in
just as one of the attackers reaches the
car.

Before she can slam the door, an arm reaches
inside, grabbing her by the hair, attempting
to pull her out of the car. Ed tries to
pull her back in. As the Woman struggles,
half in, half out — he hesitates, not
knowing whether to stop or accelerate. He
takes a swipe at the intruding arm.

```
                           ED
        Let go of her!


                         WOMAN
        Go! Just go!
```

This is the stuff that fantasy is made of — yet the crucial demand of film's hyper-reality is that the world on the screen becomes far more concrete than the daydreams of imagination. The fact is that the Thriller film story which begins with just such whims of fancy must inevitably obey boundaries of unyielding reality. Ed Okin's confusion, panic, and doubt are precisely the reactions of a normal person in such a situation, and it is his normalcy that makes the circumstance credible. For Ed to immediately leap into the heroic role of rescuer would be a violation of the fundamental Thriller character as well as the believability of the story's world. The audience knows how normal people react, knows that someone mistaken for an "international spy" has ample documentation to prove authentic identity. After all, anyone who's ever applied for a loan, entered school, or written a check has been very thoroughly vetted.

But *What if...* the bad guys refuse to recognize common sense?

THORNHILL

Not that I mind a slight case of
abduction now and then, but I do have
tickets to the theatre tonight and it
was a show I was looking forward to
and I get, well, kind of unreasonable
about things like that.

MAN

With such expert play-acting, you
make this very room a theatre.
Ah, Leonard. Have you met our
distinguished guest?

LEONARD

He's a well-tailored one, isn't he?

Thornhill give him a look of distaste.

MAN

My secretary is a great admirer of
your methods, Mr. Kaplan.
Elusiveness, however misguided —

THORNHILL
(interrupting)
Wait a minute. Did you call me
"Kaplan"?

MAN

Oh, I know you're a man of many

```
      names, but I'm perfectly willing to
      accept your current choice.

                    THORNHILL
      Current choice?  My name is Thornhill
      — Roger Thornhill — and it's never
      been anything else.

Leonard starts to chuckle. …

                    THORNHILL
      I don't suppose it would do any good
      to show you a wallet full of
      identification cards, a driver's
      license, things like that?

                    LEONARD
                (shakes his head)
      They provide you with such good
      ones.¹²
```

Well, certainly you can get to a telephone and call for help. Sooner or later the police will arrive to restore order. In fact, it is exactly these real-world, practical actions that anyone in the audience would take if they were truly faced with such an outlandish situation. So, every time the screenwriter says *What if...*, the audience will always respond, *Why don't you just....* The audience is made up of practical people who will instinctively use

---

¹² Ernest Lehman, *North by Northwest.*

the forces of society to restore reality as quickly as possible, thank their lucky stars, and then get on with their normal business. Just as surely, Thriller characters will also use the societal forces available to them. They are not heroes, but ordinary people urgently trying to extract themselves from extraordinary circumstances, just as Roger Thornhill in *North by Northwest* tries to rationally explain his predicament by seeking out the man he believes to be his kidnapper.

                    UNITED NATIONS ATTENDANT
                    This is Mr. Townsend.

Thornhill looks at the strange man, blinks
with puzzlement.

                         TOWNSEND
                    How do you do, Mr. Kaplan?

He extends his hand.

                         THORNHILL
                       (to Attendant)
                    This isn't Mr. Townsend.

                         TOWNSEND
                        (smiling)
                    Yes it is.

He holds out his hand again. Thornhill
shakes it dumbly.

                THORNHILL
     There must be... some... mistake.
     Lester Townsend?

                TOWNSEND
            (cheerfully)
     That's me. What can I do for you?

                THORNHILL
     (still utterly bewildered)
     You're the Townsend who lives in
     Glen Cove?

                TOWNSEND
     That's right. Are we neighbors?

                THORNHILL
     A large red-brick house with a
     curving tree-lined driveway?

                TOWNSEND
            (smiles)
     That's the one.

As they walk across the room, they pass a
press photographer taking flashbulb shots of
a West African group.

                    THORNHILL
Mr. Townsend, were you at home last
night?

                    TOWNSEND
You mean in Glen Cove?

                    THORNHILL
Yes.

                    TOWNSEND
No. I've been staying in my
apartment in town for the past
month. Always do when we're in
session here.

                    THORNHILL
What about Mrs. Townsend?

                    TOWNSEND
                (frowns)
My wife has been dead for many
years.

(Thornhill stares at him)

Look here, Mr. Kaplan, what's this
all about?

                    THORNHILL
Who are those people living in your
house?

               TOWNSEND
What people? The house is
completely closed up. There's just
a gardener and his wife living on
the grounds. Now, Mr. Kaplan —
suppose you tell me who you are and
what you want.

Thornhill takes the newspaper photograph
from his pocket, starts to show it to
Townsend.

               THORNHILL
Do you know this man?

Townsend glances at the picture, then
suddenly gasps and utters a strangled cry.
His eyes widen and he sags against
Thornhill, who puts his arms around him
automatically to support him.

               THORNHILL
Here. What's wrong?

Townsend groans. His eyes flutter.
Thornhill's right hand closes on the handle
of a knife protruding from Townsend's back.
Instinctively he grasps the knife, pulls it
out. Townsend slumps to the floor, dead.
Thornhill stands there in horror staring
down at him, the bloody knife upraised in

his hand. It has all happened so swiftly
that nobody has actually seen the slaying.
A woman's voice is heard crying out: "Look!"
A man's voice shouts: "What happened?"
Thornhill looks up, sees a circle of
horrified, angry faces staring at him. A
woman points at him accusingly: "He did it!
I saw him!" The group moves toward him
slowly, threateningly. Another voice cries
out: "Look out! He's got a knife!"
Thornhill backs away slowly, dazed and
confused.

                    THORNHILL
    Wait a minute now... Listen to me...
    I had nothing to do with this...

                    VOICES
    Somebody do something!... I saw
    him... Call the police!... Grab
    him!...

                    THORNHILL
    Don't come any nearer! Get back!

There is a CLICK and a FLASH OF LIGHT. The
press photographer has whipped his camera
around and caught a perfect shot of the
stunned Thornhill backing away from the
fallen body with the bloody knife still
clenched threateningly in his hand....

DAZED AND CONFUSED

In order to turn the unlikely into the credible, the Thriller writer must always acknowledge the normal — and then shut it out by excluding all possibility of resorting to rational remedies.

```
INT.  APARTMENT BUILDING — STORAGE ROOM AND
BACK DOOR

As Ed and Diana open the back door to the
alley, they find a garbage truck blocking
the doorway.  When it chugs off, Ed
discovers his car is gone.

                    ED
        My car...?

He runs after the garbage truck.  A giant
TRASH COLLECTOR is riding on the rear
platform.

                    ED
              (running and yelling)
        Wait!  Did you see a blue Toyota?

                TRASH COLLECTOR
                  (nodding)
        Couldn't get through.  Sorry 'bout
        that...

                    ED
        Where is it?
```

                    TRASH COLLECTOR
          Police towed it...

Ed is having trouble keeping up with the
truck.

                         ED
          <u>Where</u>?

                    TRASH COLLECTOR
                    (shrugs)
          Downtown, somewhere...

The truck picks up speed, leaving Ed
standing in the middle of the alley. A wave
of anger and frustration sweeps over his
frayed nerves.

                         ED
                    (yelling)
          <u>Goddamn</u> it!

Diana runs toward him. He turns and strides
past her.

                       DIANA
          Where're you going?

                         ED
          To get a taxi. I've had enough...

                    DIANA
                (following him)
        There aren't any taxis. Not at this
        hour...

                      ED
        I'll call one. I'll call one for
        you, too.

He turns into a narrow walkway between
buildings, which leads to the street. She
follows.

                    DIANA
        There's no time. I'm in a lot of
        trouble...

                      ED
        I'm the one who's in trouble, now!

                    DIANA
        They're still after me!

                      ED
        I don't think so.

                    DIANA
                (clutching him)
        Believe me — I need to get to a safe
        place, fast. I need to make some
        calls, try to straighten things
        out...

> ED
> Look, I need to get home. First, I
> need to find my car... <u>Shit</u>!

As Ed nears the front of the building and
street, Diana drops back into the shadows.

> DIANA
> (desperate)
> Please stay with me for a while
> longer… I don't want to go out
> alone. I'll pay you...

> ED
> (turning to her)
> Listen...

> DIANA
> Whatever you want. What do you
> want?

> ED
> I'm too tired for all this. I have
> to go to work in the morning.
> Sorry…

He turns away from her, steps out from
between the buildings — and stops cold.

```
ED'S POV — A WHITE MERCEDES

is parked in the driveway of the building.
The driver waits in the car while Two Men
hurry up the front steps.

                    ED
Heart pumping, he slowly backs into the
walkway, into the shadows.

                    ED
                (stunned)
        They're out in front.
```

TRAPPED IN THE MAZE

Thrillers creep up from routine life to snatch characters by the throat and yank them down into a netherworld where common sense is superfluous. The Thriller screenwriter inexorably cuts away the reassurance of the protagonist's familiar surroundings. The character is driven out of a controllable setting into the maw of an inexplicable maze where the environment is unwieldy and out of phase. In *3 Days of the Condor*, for example, Joe Turner (Robert Redford) returns from lunch to find that everyone in his office has been brutally murdered.

Turner runs downstairs on rubbery legs. He
stops at Mrs. Russell's desk, snatches up
the phone. No tone from it. Wires cut.
Holding the dead receiver, [he sees] the
cigarette she was smoking burned down nearly
the whole way before it went out.

Horrified beyond description. He moves
toward front door, stops...

EXT. ALHS HOUSE

Turner opens the door a crack, looks out to
the street. It looks normal enough.

He steps out quickly, shuts the door behind
him.

As he is going through [the door], some
unseen thing grabs him and almost pulls him
over backward.

Turner's mouth is opening to scream when he
realizes it is just his coat caught on the
gate latch. He rips it free.

TURNER'S SOLEX MOPED

The drops of rain make it sparkle.

IN THE STREET

Turner knows it would be too conspicuous.

He starts fast along the sidewalk. Madison.
Suddenly halts. Coming toward him is a
WOMAN pushing a baby carriage. She is a
dyky governess type, reflections glinting
off her thick glasses. She sees him. She
stops too, and bends over the pram to take
something out.

Covering her with the pistol in his pocket,
Turner backs across the street.

What she takes from the pram is not a
machine gun or hand grenade, but just a
baby.

TURNER

He rounds the corner running onto Madison
Avenue. Phone booth just around the corner.
It's occupied. Turner hesitates a moment,
then dashes down the block to another phone.

PHONE STAND

Turner barely manages to get the dime in.
He dials 911 automatically.

                    FILTERED VOICE
          Police Headquarters

Suddenly Turner doesn't know what to say, he
just breathes.

The labyrinth is a direct physical representation of the conundrum that the character is trying to struggle out of. The visual system of *North by Northwest*, for instance, repeats the motif of a crisscrossed puzzle. From the canted steel and glass building of the opening credits, though the streets to New York, the United Nations plaza, the Illinois corn field, and even the radical angles of Philip Vandamm's mountaintop house, Roger Thornhill is constantly imprisoned by an inescapable maze. In some cases, a bizarre setting serves to alienate the main character from the familiar even before the core dramatic conflict begins. In Alfred Hitchcock's 1955 version of *The Man Who Knew Too Much*, Jimmy Stewart as Dr. Ben McKenna, his wife Jo (Doris Day), and their son Hank are on vacation in Morocco.

```
THE BUS

The bus is entering a small Arab village.
Squat stone and plaster buildings, narrow
streets, a few carts, donkeys and one camel.
A few pedestrians, mostly Arab men, few
women.... Everything looking drab and
meager.  The sun is strong and hot....


INT. THE BUS

The bus rolls on past the Arab village into
the open desert once again.  It looks
parched and grim.
```

Tired of watching the sameness of the desert, Hank grows restless. He looks about for something to do. Ben leans back against the seat and closes his eyes. Jo takes a paper-bound novel out of her bag, finds her place. Hank decides to wander down the aisle of the bus and test its possibilities for adventure.

He rather aimlessly makes for the front of the bus. Having left the Arab village, the bus picks up speed, and is beginning to bump and sway somewhat. When Hank is a little better than half way down the aisle, the bus sways in a particularly startling manner, causing Hank to stagger. In order to steady himself, he thrusts out his hand to grab the side of a seat. He misses the seat, and only succeeds in clutching at the veil of an Arab woman. Unfortunately, he pulls the veil from her face.

The startled woman, instantly horrified, covers her face with her hands and gives a sharp cry.

With the bus still bumping and swaying, Hank staggers a bit without realizing that he still has hold of the woman's veil.

The woman still covers her face, but from the seat next to her, an Arab rises and makes a sharp comment in Arabic to Hank.... He starts to move past the woman toward Hank, repeating his demand... assaulting the boy in furious Arabic....

Ben rises quickly and advances protectively toward his son and the oncoming Arab.

Of course, when the physical reality changes for the main character, the sudden loss of normalcy begins the process of mental and emotional bewilderment as well, making an appropriate response to the new reality nearly impossible, as Joe Turner experiences in *3 Days of the Condor*.

INT.   A SMALL ROOM SOMEWHERE

Windowless. Could be anywhere. No sense of place, but a perfect sense of time: Clocks run around the walls, heading time-zones on the wall-maps.

            TURNER (V.O.)
   ...Hello?

Coming from a massive speaker hung from the ceiling.

A legless man in a wheelchair — MITCHELL —
is alert, leaning forward. He fine-tunes
knobs on a bank of communications equipment
before him. Tape recorders are already
turning... then speaks into a talk-box.

                    MITCHELL
          This is the Major.

                    TURNER (V.O.)
          This is Joe Turner! Listen...

                    MITCHELL
          Identification.

                    TURNER (V.O.)
          What??

EXT.   PHONE BOX AND TURNER

Passersby seem menacing to Turner.

                    TURNER
          I told you, my name's <u>Turner</u> — I
          work for you! Something's happened,
          somebody came in and —

                    MITCHELL
          Identify yourself.

Turner can only hold tight to the phone, his
mind blank.

69

Coming to grips with the altered reality requires the character to assess conflicting emotional information in the light of physical evidence, such as when Allie (Bridget Fonda) uncovers the proof of the duplicity of her roommate Hedy (Jennifer Jason Leigh) in *Single White Female*.

INT.   ALLIE'S APARTMENT — HEDY'S ROOM — NIGHT

Allie rifles through the drawers of Hedy's nightstand. She roots through her dresser, spreads all of Hedy's purses on the bed, ransacks all of them. In the closet, she checks in all of Hedy's jacket pockets. On the top shelf, she sees a shoebox. She takes this down, carries it to the bed. She opens it.

INSIDE THE SHOEBOX

A bundle of letters, rubber-banded together. But they're not addressed to Hedra Carlson. Instead, the older ones are addressed to "ELLEN BESCH" on Copeland Drive, Tampa, Florida.... There's also a small blank white envelope, unsealed. Allie upends it and four scraps of photographic paper fall onto the bed: A snapshot has been shredded. Allie assembles the photo slowly. When she's finished, she sees a family group

taken in the early seventies. An ordinary
family posed in front of a suburban house: a
mother, a father, two little girls —
presumably twins, because they're the same
height and dressed exactly alike. But the
face of one of the girls has been scratched
off with a razor....

ALLIE

puzzled, angry — and afraid. She quickly
puts everything back...

Even humorous encounters, like Roger Thornhill's eccentric
attempt to shave with Eve's miniature safety-razor in Chicago's
La Salle Street Train Station men's room, serve to divorce the
main character from reality that much more, as he attempts to
preserve normalcy while on the run for his life.

INT. MEN'S ROOM

There is considerable activity here. At the
row of wash basins stand three men. One is
washing his hands, the other is scraping
away at his chin with a straight razor, and
the third man — Thornhill — is busily
rubbing in a foamy lather which covers the
lower half of his face.... Suddenly the door

```
bursts open and two detectives enter....
Thornhill nonchalantly finishes his
lathering, then looks down and picks up his
razor.  It is the tiny one belonging to Eve.
In the mirror he catches sight of the man
with the straight razor staring at him in
bewilderment.
```

Available space itself tends to contract and become confused as the main character moves deeper and deeper into off-kilter surroundings. *Wait Until Dark* traps the blind Suzy Hendrix (Audrey Hepburn) in her now terrifying basement apartment, a labyrinth she can no longer negotiate because her furniture landmarks have been jumbled out of place. Likewise, in *Single White Female*, Allie's world begins in a roomy New York flat that is literally too large for her to handle alone. But as Allie's psychotic roommate Hedy voraciously consumes Allie's identity, the physical surroundings lose substance as well. The apartment building itself becomes a bizarre maze of darkened corridors, indistinct voices, and locked doors until the final life-or-death scene is played out in the dungeon of the cellar.

As the Thriller story progresses, then, what seems at first to be open space available for the threatened protagonist to escape, quickly takes on the confusion and the terror of unknown territory, steadily contracting into a harshly inhibited environment where hunter and hunted lay siege to each other in a desperate act of survival.

Francois Truffaut
... in *North by Northwest* all of the shots are
of equal duration.

Alfred Hitchcock
Here you're not dealing with time but with
space. The length of the shots was to
indicate the various distances that a man had
to run for cover and, more than that, to
show that there was no cover to run to.[13]

Naturally, the film director is responsible for establishing the Thriller's visual setting with the moving pictures on the screen — but it is the screenwriter who must first provide the *imagery* of words on the page that create the tone of the Thriller's bounded world.

THE DEMOLITION OF REALITY

This obliteration of the familiar physical world also forces the protagonist to struggle for a foothold on the bewildering inner landscape where the old landmarks of common sense are no longer visible.

Anyone who has ever experienced an earthquake knows the shockingly abrupt loss of contact with the most consistent, solid base of life, the very ground we walk on. Not only is there the immediate danger caused by falling objects and the distraction of noise, darkness, and motion, but on a psychological level there is the terrifying loss of control over the world. Long after the initial tremor has subsided, earthquake victims, even though

---

[13] Francois Truffaut, HITCHCOCK, (Simon and Schuster, 1966).

they have not been physically harmed at all, experience enormous upheaval to their sense of well-being. Their ability to predict, not what the future will bring, but whether or not there will, indeed, be a future sometimes seems used up.[14]

It is exactly this struggle between the mind's truth and the direct experience of the physical world that Thriller films make the most of. In *Breakdown*, for example, Jeff (Kurt Russell) and Amy (Kathleen Quinlan) Taylor find themselves stranded in the middle of a desert during a cross-country move. Amy catches a ride into a nearby diner with Red (J.T. Walsh), a goodhearted trucker, in order to call for help. But when Jeff finally follows her into town, she's not there, and when he catches up with Red, Jeff's reality is abruptly jerked out from under him.

```
EXT. DESERT HIGHWAY
The Cherokee crests a hill... and then in
the distance, he sees it...

THE PETERBILT
The 18-wheeler that picked up Amy.  Cruising
leisurely.  Jeff presses the accelerator...

EXT.  DESERT HIGHWAY
The Cherokee gains rapidly on the Peterbilt
and comes up behind.

INT. CHEROKEE — DAY
Jeff honks his horn, flashes his lights.
```

---

[14] Although Thrillers often deal with the tortured perception of reality, the stories generally do not dramatize actual mental illness, as do films like *A Beautiful Mind*.

> JEFF
> C'mon you fat-ass. Pull over.

Either the driver doesn't notice, or he's ignoring Jeff, but the truck does not slow down.

Jeff shifts into the oncoming lane and pulls alongside the cab. He honks again and waves, gesturing for the truck to pull over. But the Peterbilt maintains its speed.

Jeff cranes his neck to get a glimpse of the driver...

It's Red alright (sic). But he's wearing a different cap.

Red peers down at Jeff, puzzled. Jeff shouts back at him, waves.

> JEFF
> Pull over! Pull over!

Red suddenly notices something ahead in the road, blares his horn.

Jeff looks up, sees —

An RV CAMPER approaching in the oncoming lane!

HIGHWAY
Jeff slams on his brakes and swerves behind
the Peterbilt, not a moment too soon, as the
RV whooshes past in the opposite direction,
horn blaring.

CHEROKEE
Jeff is rattled, catching his breath, but
stays right behind the truck. He checks to
see if the oncoming lane is clear, then
swings out to pass again, overtaking the
Peterbilt.

He slips in ahead, then starts weaving and
braking, forcing the truck to slow.

HIGHWAY
Both vehicles pull to the side of the road
and stop. Jeff leaps out of the Cherokee
and runs over as Red climbs down from the
cab.

The cab is empty.

                    RED
          Jesus, pal, what the hell
          you doing?

                    JEFF
          I was signaling for you to stop.
          Didn't you see me?

                    RED
        No.

Jeff reacts. How thick can this guy be?

                    JEFF
        Where's my wife?

                    RED
        Huh?

                    JEFF
        My wife. Where is she?

Red gives him a puzzled look.

                    RED
        How should I know where your
        wife is?

                    JEFF
        I checked at the diner. No one
        saw her there.

                    RED
        Mister, I don't know what you're
        talking about.

Jeff stares — is this guy nuts?

                    JEFF
      You gave her a ride. You were
      supposed to drop her at Belle's
      diner.

Red searches his memory, trying to be as
helpful as possible. He shakes his head.

                    RED
      Nope. Sorry.

                    JEFF
      How can you not remember? It
      was just half an hour ago for
      crissakes!

Red gives him a peculiar look.

                    RED
      Mister, I never seen you before
      in my life.

The audience is caught up in the lead character's nightmare
because they, themselves, have witnessed the events that Jeff
believes to be true, so they can empathize with his frustration at
the denial of that truth. At the same time, the audience has a
shudder of dread that such a terrifying shift in reality could
easily happen to them. The fact that anyone who has stopped
on a lonely road in the middle of nowhere has had the fleeting
thought that, in the right circumstances, they or a loved one
could disappear without a trace injects a potent hypodermic of

authentic reality directly into the fiction of the film, and thereby turns the make-believe all the more real.

The serum can easily wear off, however, because the audience is keenly aware that the everyday world is filled with checks and balances, as well as appeals to levels of authority and systems of verification. The scriptwriter must constantly husband the resources of the screenplay to sustain that precarious equilibrium between the audience's acceptance of the imaginary reality and the incursion of the true-life world.

PLEA FOR REASSURANCE – FAITH AGAINST REASON

From Kant to quanta we've learned that our individual perceptions of reality are dependent on maintaining a more or less consistent repetition of familiar patterns. If those perceptions land wide of the reality mark, as they do after the initial trauma in a Thriller, the character's first action is to squeeze the brakes on the disorienting bewilderment by reaffirming the regular layout of life. Surely there must be another human being who can testify that the world hasn't changed, that life is normal, and that the adverse event is merely a temporary deviation from the prescribed path. When life goes awry because of a natural disaster, a divorce, a loss of job, or some other distress, we seek the natural reparative mechanism of talking to friends or social groups, or even professional counselors, until we're able to incorporate the disturbing events into our scheme of reality. Ordinarily, we come to grips with the trauma, but in fact, nothing has changed in the real world. The only change is in our relationship to the perceptual universe. In a Thriller, however, the adjustment to a new perception is not that easy, because instead of a single traumatic event that must be incorporated into the scheme of life, the Thriller protagonist is continually barraged by nerve-shattering attacks with little or no time to assimilate their meaning.

          ROBERT CLAYTON DEAN
    Why are they after me?

          BRILL
    You have something they want.

          ROBERT CLAYTON DEAN
    I don't have anything!...

          BRILL
    ...If you live another day, I'll
    be very impressed![15]

Thrillers, like the slow-motion nightmares of childhood, surround you with the relentless terror that someone is determined to take your life away, and that no matter how fast or how far you run, you cannot possibly escape.

---

[15] *Enemy of the State*

Scribble Exercise:

Tom, a metal worker (blacksmith, ironmonger, welder, sculptor, factory riveter, etc.) is kidnapped from his bed one night by four mysterious men. Tom is blindfolded and taken to a secret location where he is forced to use his skills to construct an oddly-shaped scaffold. In the course of his work, Tom learns that as soon as he has finished, the men intend to kill him, but at an opportune moment he manages to escape. Tom cannot return home to his wife and family because he is certain the men will be watching his house. He also cannot go to the authorities because he has recognized one of his kidnappers as the head of local law enforcement.

❏ **What do each of these Bounded World contexts provide for this Thriller premise? Which one provides the most effective Thriller context?**

- Paris, France – 1793
- Washington, D.C. – 1865
- New York City - 1929
- Kansas City, MO - 2003
- Fenyman, Mars - 2150

❏ **What are the specific Bounded World limitations for this Thriller story?**

❏ **How do those limitations constrain the action of the story into a Cosmos of Credibility?**

❏ **What objects, locations, mechanisms, or paraphernalia would violate the Cosmos of Credibility?**

CHAPTER 6

TIMESCAPE

Referred to in *Screenwriting 101: The Essential Craft of Feature Film Writing* and *Writing the Action-Adventure Film: The Moment of Truth* as the Plausible Moment, the concept of time within the Cosmos of Credibility is not merely that of a particular clock-ticking interval, but a much more universal moment that runs from the discernible to the barely noticeable.

In the first place there is, of course, the Projection Time, or the literal length of the movie measured in actual screen minutes. For the most part, the audience is not concerned about this measure of time at all, unless the film has an especially long running time. If the movie is more than two hours in length, the audience — no matter how much they may enjoy the film — is likely to ask why such an extended time was necessary. In turn, this means that every scene must give the audience *new information* about the story, must thrust the story forward so that the audience's Perceived Story Time makes the film seem to be much shorter than its literal running time.

Thrillers, by their nature, exist in highly compressed time. The audience has a sense of Reality Time just as they have of real-world space, that cannot be stretched beyond a limit of credibility. For this reason, a three-hour Thriller would be nearly impossible to sustain. Thrillers do not demand epic scope, a multiplicity of characters, or lengthy enactments of social and political forces. Both *Gladiator* and *Ben-Hur* are about men who are mistakenly and unjustly torn from their everyday reality, betrayed by their societies, and threatened by conspiracies of evil, yet neither of these films would be at all credible as Thrillers because they make use of an entirely different Era-Event concept of time that emphasizes the historical/political trappings.

The true Thriller, on the other hand, relies on a rapid narrative technique that creates for the audience a very swift Perceived Story Time. Regardless of the supposed timeline of the story, three days in *3 Days of the Condor*, several weeks in *Arlington Road*, or only a few hours as in *Breakdown*, all Thrillers *seem* to take place over extremely compressed time spans — because the audience inherently knows that the Thriller's requirement of acute physical or social isolation that cuts the protagonist off from outside help forces the genre into a very short but intense Timescape. Longer perceived times would significantly lessen the credibility of the events that are contrived to create the Thriller plot.

TIME OUT OF MIND

However, there is one area of the Timescape in a Thriller that is more plastic: the Potential Time of the main character's rational perceptions. Most days for most people are reasonably predictable. As a matter of fact, predictability has always been a goal of the human race, as evidenced by artifacts from the giant stone calendars of the Maya and Stonehenge through Henry Ford's reliable assembly line to today's long-range weather forecasts. As much as we may gripe about the sameness of our jobs or the unavoidable daily traffic, we actually need a sense of an expected future in order to remain sane.

84

FEAR IS PAIN ARISING FROM THE ANTICIPATION OF EVIL.

– Aristotle

But what if there is no future? What if the mind is so engorged with fear that it cannot even conceive of tomorrow? What if there is only an unrelieved, excruciating, adrenaline-garroted *now*? The human panic reaction occurs in an observable, unremitting progression where successively more primitive areas of the brain take over the responsibility for controlling behavior until the sense of time is virtually destroyed.[16]

CALM	AROUSAL	ALARM	FEAR	TERROR
NEOCORTEX	SUBCORTEX	LIMBIC	MIDBRAIN	BRAINSTREAM
EXTENDED FUTURE	DAYS/HOURS	HOURS/ MINUTES	MINUTES/ SECONDS	LOSS OF SENSE OF TIME

This tyranny of fear causes even the most rational characters to act irrationally as the reptilian brain of survival knocks the rational brain out of the box.

The bathtub scene in *Marathon Man* demonstrates the power that raw fear exerts not only on a character, but on the audience engaged in the scene.

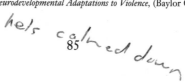

Dick writes from the neo.cortex. Dick is Horse lover fat after

hels calmed down

---

[16] Bruce D. Perry, M.D., Ph.D., *Neurodevelopmental Adaptations to Violence*, (Baylor College of Medicine, 1996).

Babe in the tub... as he sinks into
reverie... and [then] comes one of the most
frightening things that you can ever hear:
whispering. Babe lies there an instant,
listening, as out of sight in his room the
whispering comes again.

Then he dives for the door, slams it shut
fast, locks it. He stands there breathing
hard, eyes wide. From beyond the door now:
a sound: 'click.'

Babe turns out the bathroom light. Light
from the main room comes in under the door.
There is another 'click' sound and the light
from the next room is dimmer. 'Click.'
Dimmer yet. It's terrifying. Another
'click.' Then there is no more light coming
in under the door.

Babe turns the lights the hell back on in
the bathroom, grabs for his pajamas, gets
into them. Silence for a moment. Then a
different sound: 'scratch; scratch.'

Someone is starting to pull and twist the
hinges from the bathroom door. Babe stares
a moment, then whirls, opens the cabinet,
but there's nothing but an electric razor
and toothpaste.

There are three hinges on the door and now
the bottom one is pulled out. Without a
pause, the middle hinge begins to twist.
There is no window in the room, no place to
go.

                    BABE
          Anybody — <u>Listen</u> —
          <u>-- Get the goddam cops!</u> —

... Babe... is moving to the door, his hand
on the knob as the third hinge continues to
move and when it's out the door will be
freed and Babe goes right on shouting —

                    BABE
          Help — somebody save me for Jesus
          sakes — Please somebody — ANYBODY
          SAVE ME — DO SOMETHING — PLEEESE.

The last hinge slides free and the second it
does —

Babe yanks the door in and dives for his
desk and as the door is freed we can see
whoever's out there and it's the LIMPER who
mugged Elsa, and Babe shoulders him aside
but now, suddenly —

THE MAMMOTH, moving out of the darkness and
Babe is candy, because before he can even

```
try for the desk drawer the Mammoth has him
and with terrible power shoves him down and
before Babe can rise the Mammoth is on him
and he lifts Babe and throws him toward the
light of the bathroom…

Babe, crashing down, stunned, trying to
move, but the Mammoth forces him back and
into the tub.  …He's holding Babe under…
```

The fact, however, is that there is no logical reason for the Limper and the Mammoth to bring the tools necessary to pry the bathroom door from its hinges. It would be far more sensible to simply wait until Babe exits the bathroom, conk him out, and then cart him away to Szell's lair. Furthermore, having broken down the bathroom door, they have their victim completely at their mercy, so there is absolutely no justification for upending the helpless Babe into the bath water. *Rationally*, their actions truly make no sense.

Similarly, the know-nothing charade that the trucker Red puts on for Jeff Taylor in *Breakdown* is truly not necessary. Since Red and his cohorts fully intend to shake down Jeff for his wife's ransom, there is no rational reason to go through the sham of pretense. However, logic is not in play on the table here. The set-up of *Breakdown* makes Red's actions seem to be reasonable, and therefore all the more frightening for both the main character and the audience.

IS IT SAFE?

Rationality is a function of the cortex where life's decisions are weighed and measured. But when the cortex has been devoured by the voracious reptile of the brainstem, terror consumes reasonableness, forethought, and even time itself, so that unalloyed fear becomes the *only* reality. The predictability of life's agenda has been so deformed by fear that the character has only the incessant trepidation of the present. In this condition, confidence in self-awareness is shattered. The cardinal points of the internal compass no longer point true, so that it is impossible to assemble a coherent response to an unreasonable universe.

```
Babe, semi-conscious, wearing pajamas, damp.
He sits in a chair, the chair is in a
windowless room.[17]

Babe blinks, tries to get a better look at
the place, but he's expertly bound to the
chair.  The room seems unusually bright.
There is a sink, a table; it all seems
clean.  There come sounds from behind him
and the Limper and the Mammoth walk around
the chair.  The Mammoth carries an armload
of clean white towels, beautifully folded.

The BALD MAN moving toward the chair,
carrying a rolled up towel in one hand.  He
```

---

[17] *Marathon Man*

indicates that he wants the lamp brought
closer. The Limper hurriedly obeys; the
Bald Man turns quickly, washes his hands.
As he does —

                    BALD MAN
        Is it safe?

                      BABE
        Huh?

                    BALD MAN
        Is it safe?

                      BABE
        Is what safe?

                    BALD MAN
        Is it safe?

                      BABE
        I don't know what you mean.

                    BALD MAN
        Is it safe?

                      BABE
        I can't tell you if something's
        safe or not unless I know
        specifically what you're
        asking about.

                    BALD MAN
          Is it safe?

                      BABE
          -- tell me what the 'it'
          refers to.

                    BALD MAN
          Is it safe?

                      BABE
          Yes, it's very safe — it's so
          safe you wouldn't believe it.
          There; now you know.

                    BALD MAN
          Is it safe?

                      BABE
          No, it isn't safe. Very
          dangerous; be careful.

For a moment the Bald Man stares down at
Babe. There is a terrible intelligence
working inside. Now a nod. Just one, as
he unwraps the towel and we see the
contents: dental tools.

In the best of Thrillers, the main character's reality Timescape
is permanently altered as a result of the story. In *3 Days of the*

91

Condor, although Joe Turner has managed to escape for the moment by turning over incriminating evidence to the *New York Times*, in his final confrontation with Higgins (Cliff Robertson), Turner recognizes with sudden irony that the remainder of his life will be marked by an ominous clock.

                    HIGGINS
          You've done more damage than you
          know.

                    TURNER
          I hope so.

                    HIGGINS
          You're about to be a very lonely
          man, Turner.

Without warning, Turner slowly starts away, still facing Higgins. He throws a glance over his shoulder at the car [where the two men wait for a signal from Higgins].

                    HIGGINS
          It didn't have to turn out like
          this.

                    TURNER
          Of course it did.

                    HIGGINS
        Turner! How do you know they'll
        print it?

Turner stops. Stares at Higgins. Higgins
smiles.

                    HIGGINS
        You can take a walk. But how
        far? If they don't print it.

                    TURNER
        They'll print it.

Pedestrians move between them

                    HIGGINS
        How do you know?

Trapped in a hyper-vigilant *now* like a drowning victim, the Thriller character flails about for a reliable buoy to cling to. Surely there must be a wife, a lover, a friend, or an institution that can reconfirm familiar reality; some rescuer who will lead the way out of the labyrinth.

But it is exactly this desperate prayer for a return to normalcy that hurls the Thriller protagonist into the most bitter waters of acid terror.

Scribble Exercise:

❏ **What elements influence the Timescape in these films?**

- *Alien*
- *Cape Fear*
- *Jagged Edge*
- *The Man Who Knew Too Much*
- *Single White Female*

❏ **The closer a Thriller's Timescape is to real-world time, the more fear-provoking it is for an audience. Why?**

CHAPTER 7

CHARACTER ETHOS

The Greek *ethos* from which we derive the word *ethic* refers to the natural endowment or distinctive spirit of a people, as well as to the traits of a person influenced by that culture. In drama, it is a set of principles of right conduct that a character exhibits in everyday behaviors.

It is these fundamental moral choices that define the *protagonist*, or lead character of a drama, and the *antagonist*, or dramatic opposition. Just as people in everyday life make choices from the trivial to the crucial, based on their best guess of how those choices will influence their lives, so do characters in a drama. The greater the personal or the financial risk, the more a person will normally dwell on the decision, and will ordinarily choose the minimum action necessary to achieve what is wanted. No one ever voluntarily takes a truly big risk, not only because such a risk would put finances, domestic happiness, or even freedom in jeopardy, but because guessing wrong would mean having to readjust a carefully protected self-image.

Although dramatic characters are motivated by the same ethos as real-life people, drama itself is *not* life. Drama is life intensified. The screenwriter constructs situations for a dramatic character where it is impossible to avoid a momentous consequence of choice. But, the choice will not produce the expected results for the character or the audience, and that unanticipated result will force the character to make yet another

95

difficult decision, which will also not produce the predicted result, and so forth until the conflict between the main character and the antagonist reaches a point where the main character *must* come to grips with the self-concept in order to resolve the external problem in a decisive way. Put simply, it is the hard choices a character must make that are the *dramatic action* of the story.

Everything in a drama is active through cause-and-effect plausibility. The physical actions of the characters are driven by their obsession to reach the exterior goal. Whether their physical actions are successful or not depends on the difficult choices those characters make — and the choices are driven, in turn, by the character's self-concepts as shaped by inner needs. Without this dramatic action of making difficult decisions, there is absolutely nothing to move the Narrative Trajectory forward. If characters are simply shoved into physical action for no legitimate reason, the story becomes a mere list of stunts. No matter how inventive or how engaging each gag may be, it is not dramatic because the actions are not performed in the service of a decision. Quite literally, *nothing happens.*

Thriller films require the making of choices that explore the main character's doubts and weaknesses of "What should I do?" At the same time, the audience is also trying to figure out how they would respond in the same circumstances because the choices arise from a shared ethos, which keeps the audience intensely identified with the protagonist's dilemma.

Dick's stories are Thrillers, but the narrative voice is at all times ironic, never increasing the fear, but upping the absurdity of power politics. The Antagonist is POWERFUL but DELUDED.

96

Dick loves Berkeley, like Twain loved the Mississippi, but he laughs at things that would outrage most. Most of all, he makes fun of outrage.

THRILLER PROTAGONISTS

1. **The Thriller protagonist is an *Everyman* thrust into an extreme situation.** This character allows the audience to experience their own nightmares as they focus their emotional identification on the character's willingness to stay alive. While Thrillers and Action-Adventures have many superficial elements in common, there is one very clear distinguishing characteristic that separates the two genres. The Thriller protagonists are ordinary, everyday people who are completely unprepared for the devastating circumstances that they are plunged into, while the protagonists of Action-Adventures have an ethos of physical, mental, and moral preparation that compels them to deliberately engage the overpowering opposition. *Alien* is a Thriller about a group of interstellar truck drivers who find themselves caught in a terrifying maze with no possibility of escape or help. The protagonists of the Action-Adventure *Aliens*, on the other hand, are hard-core Marines who have the sanctioned duty of a specific mission and are fully aware of the danger they face. Of course, the Thriller protagonist may be an unusual, even skilled person in a particular walk of life, but the character is a relative *naif* with respect to the threat faced in the Thriller story.

2. **The Thriller protagonist does not possess martial skills.** Although the character may have useful skills not directly related to the situation, he is not an expert in hand-to-hand combat, firearms, or any other life-saving lethal skill. In *3 Days of the Condor*, Joe Turner's CIA dossier mentions that he worked in telecommunications while serving in the Army. Turner's knowledge of system patches, then, becomes an element in his ability to confound his

This outrage is the urge to seek power.

Hollywood has screwed up every Dick adaptation, because they aim to thrill us, and Dick just won't be afraid.

pursuers by cross-connecting the lines during his telephone calls to them.

3. **The Thriller protagonist does not come equipped with official sanction.** Unlike the protagonist of an Action-Adventure, who enters the story generally as some kind of military or police presence with the official consent and duty to engage the enemy, the protagonist of a Thriller is an ordinary person thrown into extraordinary circumstances. The character, therefore, is not certified by any authorized "license to kill." It is an important distinction because the Thriller protagonist acts *in absentia* for the audience and must therefore act with the ethos of the audience. In other words, no matter how dire the circumstances, the character can only kill in a life-threatening situation of self-defense or defense of others. The character must be deputized *by the audience*, and the power to kill is therefore limited to those situations where the audience itself would, in real life, be willing to pull the trigger.

4. **The Thriller protagonist is baffled by the dilemma.** The strongest initial reaction of the Thriller main character is total disbelief. In *North by Northwest*, by sheerest coincidence Roger Thornhill summons the same hotel bellboy who has been paging for a Mr. George Kaplan.

Thornhill takes a pen and a long envelope from his inside pocket as he addresses the bellboy.

Dick won't fear because he knows God, and this whole world is nonsense. Like one of th Outlaws of the Marsh, he laughs at danger.

THORNHILL
Look, I've got to get a wire off
immediately. Can you send it for me
if I write it out for you?

BELLBOY
I'm not permitted to do that, sir,
but if you'll follow me —

THORNHILL
(to the others at the table)
Will you excuse me for a moment?

WADE
Go right ahead....

Thornhill walks off with the bell boy....

OUTSIDE THE OAK BAR

Thornhill and the bellboy emerge from the
room.

BELLBOY
(pointing)
Right there, sir.

THORNHILL
Thanks.

Thornhill starts toward the Western Union
office as the bellboy goes off in another

"The greatest fear is fear of the unknown" H. P. Lovecraft.

*Dick knows no fear, only laughter.
The ~~protagonist~~ narrator is a harmless sociopath.*

direction. Suddenly two "unobtrusive" men
walk swiftly directly behind Thornhill....
One of them taps him on the shoulder. He
pauses and turns.

                    THORNHILL
     Yes.

                    FIRST MAN
     The car is waiting outside. You
     will walk between us saying nothing.

                    THORNHILL
     What are you talking about?

                    SECOND MAN
               (taking Thornhill's arm)
     Let's go.

                    THORNHILL
     Go where? Who are you?

                    FIRST MAN
     Mere errand boys, carrying concealed
     weapons. His is pointed at your
     heart, so please, no errors of
     judgment, I beg of you.

                    THORNHILL
               (pulling free)
     What is this — a joke or something?

```
                    SECOND MAN
          Yes.   A joke.
```

He removes his hand from his pocket, shoves a gun into Thornhill's ribs

```
                    SECOND MAN
          We will laugh in the car.
```

Thornhill stares at the man for a moment.

```
                    THORNHILL
          This is ridiculous.
```

This stubborn "Why me?" incredulity, the reluctance to accept the sudden change in reality, is precisely the attitude that places the character in mortal danger. The protagonist's refusal to accept the radically altered world, and the insistence on regaining normalcy, is a compulsion that digs the character deeper into the dangerous maze. Because of Professor Michael Faraday's (Jeff Bridges) tenacious refusal to accept the painful reality of his wife's death in *Arlington Road*, he injects himself into a world of danger that is so far beyond his capacity to directly confront that he loses his hold on ordinary reality with particularly tragic consequences. Because Allie in *Single White Female* refuses to accept that she greatly misjudged the roommate she felt such an affinity for, Hedy's psychosis revs well into the red zone before Allie realizes she's in danger.

Narrative Voice

The Protagonist in Dick
is laughing at the absurdity
of power itself.

5. **The Thriller protagonist is a dabbler in life, a person who is marked by the avoidance of commitment.** It is difficult to cast an iron mold for all Thriller protagonists, but by and large the lead characters in Thrillers share a common ethos of evasion and nonconfrontation. The Thriller protagonist has developed strategic avoidance as the principal skill for coping with the pressures of daily life. In the beginning of *North by Northwest*, Roger Oliver Thornhill is presented as a glib, sophisticated advertising executive dictating notes to his faithful secretary. He even has her sending flowers to his mother. This character who states that he has "three ex-wives and several bartenders" depending on him, clearly is not someone to rely on for stability. Joe Turner in *3 Days of the Condor* is a dodger. When it's his turn to pick up lunch for the office, rather than take the normal route, he slips out the back through a short-cut hole in the fence. Indeed, the action saves him from assassination, but it is also indicative of the uncommitted style of his life. A telling scene early in *Marathon Man* gives an important clue to Babe's character. While jogging in Central Park, Babe takes up the challenge of a stronger runner, but when the going gets tough, instead of pumping harder, Babe gives up the race altogether. In this instance the consequences of his letdown are minor, but in the story to come the pay-off for lack of resolve is death. Virtually every Thriller begins with a main character who is somehow incomplete, lacking an essential commitment to life or in the self-sufficient confidence to meet life head-on. It is precisely this inadequacy that will be severely tested in the process of the Thriller.

How do Dick's characters fare?

6. **The Thriller protagonist has the simple objective of trying to stay alive.** Because the Thriller protagonist is

more or less self-centered and, moreover, because the character is directly threatened by the antagonist, the primary goal is to escape death. It is this Narrative Trajectory that the screenwriter must never lose sight of. If the audience cares about anything, they care about how the protagonist is going to remain alive. Any diversion from the Narrative Trajectory of escaping death tries the patience of the audience and ultimately stretches their fundamental suspension of disbelief.

7. **The Thriller protagonist discovers that personal salvation is also the only method to save society from a larger menace or conspiracy.** The nature of the Thriller antagonist is such that, nearly always, the menace threatening the protagonist is merely a sample of a greater danger to society at large. Joe Turner in *3 Days of the Condor* uncovers a secret CIA plot. Babe in *Marathon Man* is caught up in a conspiracy of Nazi evil. Roger Thornhill in *North by Northwest* has stumbled into a nest of international espionage agents. Even in the relatively tight Thrillers such as *Wait Until Dark* and *Single White Female*, the protagonists are the only people who can stop the evil from spreading to the community at large. For the Thriller audience, this expanded threat is crucial. As much as they may identify with the predicament of the main character, it is the extension of the threat into the "real" world that is truly frightening. It would be too bad if the hero dies, but, after all, that's only one person. However, if that one person is the only thing standing between the antagonist and the world at large, the hero's fight for life becomes much more worthwhile. Unfortunately, not all Thrillers take this requirement as sincerely as they might. *Enemy of the State*, for instance, for all the menace of its set-up, ultimately

degenerates into an ending that substitutes pandering comedy for courage, and results in a shootout among buffoons that is entirely unworthy of the powerful societal threat presented by the force of the antagonist.

8. **The Thriller protagonist has untested personal courage, honor, or principles.** This is not to say that the Thriller protagonist is a coward, but that there is a significant difference between the nature of Thriller back-to-the-wall courage motivated by self interest, and the Action-Adventure courage of moral conviction motivated by principle. It is another distinction between the Action-Adventure and Thriller genres that the Action-Adventure protagonist gains courage because of moral conviction, whereas the Thriller protagonist gains moral conviction because of courage.

A fascinating contrast plays out in *Marathon Man* when the Nazi death-camp doctor Szell is forced to prowl through the New York diamond district to hock his fistful of gemstones amidst the very Jews he once tortured.

```
An ANCIENT OLD CRONE bent and trembling,
across the street.  She holds out one
trembling hand pointing it dead at Szell,
standing there crying out with whatever
strength is left to her —

                   CRONE
        DER WEISSE ENGEL — SZELL — SZELL

SZELL. It takes everything he has not to
break into a wild panicked run.  But he
doesn't.  He turns away from the screaming
```

crone, takes up his pace again, heading as
before toward 6th Avenue as the word 'Szell'
continues to be hurled into the steaming
air.

Bathed in sweat now, but under control, not
bolting, making his steady way but even
then —

An OLD MAN WITH A BEARD. He hesitates,
listens, looks around —

> OLD BEARDED MAN
> Szell? -- Szell is here? —

Another OLD MAN turning around too.

> OLD MAN
> -- <u>where is Szell?</u>

The Crone still screaming, still pointing
her fingers, her gnarled trembling hand
following Szell's movement —

> CRONE
> (louder, still)
> -- <u>nein — nein —</u>
> <u>DER WEISSE ENGEL IST HIER ! ! !</u>

At the same time, Babe, who has spent his life avoiding
responsibility of any kind so as not to test his lack of courage,
has been driven by desperation to save his life, and consequently

into a moral commitment not merely to hunt down the despotic Nazi, but to force him into degradation in the filth of a sewer.

Szell drops to his knees by the stairs, puts down his briefcase. Behind him now are strange lights, dim, and dripping water....

The fortune [in diamonds] practically overflows the case...

> SZELL
> Leave me a little, that's my only request. Enough, whatever you think fair.

> BABE
> Fair? — I'm surprised you even know that word. What've you done in your life that was fair?

> SZELL
> 30 years ago — what I did was half a lifetime behind me, there is in law, a statute of limitations — you are a scholar, when do you allow it to run out? You are very young — brilliant, yes, but not yet wise -- ...

[Babe] raises the pistol, cocks it. And Szell folds. He just grows old as we watch, old and pleading and helpless.

> SZELL
> Why do you need my life? What
> do I have left? Five years? Five
> years in a jungle, hiding, always,
> always in fear. What is so
> glorious about that for you to
> take it away, when in return I
> offer you a life of dreams.

It's really pathetic, seeing him go to
pieces like that, until his right hand goes
in motion, the knife already sliding into
killing position and as he starts his swipe,
a gunshot explodes and Szell staggers back a
moment, and for a moment, he cannot believe
what has happened.

Babe. Very calm, the gun in his hand, ready
to fire again. He's a long way now from
the distraught kid we met early on.

THE THRILLER ANTAGONIST

1. **The Thriller antagonist is morally different.** Drama is
   about opposition, conflict. Someone fights against someone
   else for a *reason*. The reason has to do with the character's
   ethos. While the protagonist is, indeed, trying to escape
   death, the choices available do not include the same options
   as those of the antagonist. Because the antagonist comes
   from a different moral ethos, however, the single-minded
   pursuit of a goal permits any action, including murder, in the
   achievement of that goal.

107

2. **The Thriller antagonist creates an unremitting climate of fear.** The antagonist drives the Thriller forward by the relentless pursuit of a goal. The interference of the protagonist, then, becomes more than a mere annoyance, but the potential destruction of the antagonist. The antagonist must permanently prohibit the main character from obstructing the goal.

3. **The Thriller antagonist is willing to kill.** The antagonist's moral code permits the destruction of anyone who interferes with the goal. For the main character, killing is an act that, however much it may be in self defense, must seem to the audience to be morally justified on the part of the protagonist. The antagonist, on the other hand, has no such strictures. If the antagonist were subject to the same moral strictures as the protagonist, then there would be no conflict between the two characters

4. **The Thriller antagonist is extremely powerful.** The antagonist is representative of a larger conspiracy or threat of some kind, an imminent scheme that endangers not only the protagonist, but the community at large — including, by extension, the audience. In *3 Days of the Condor*, the secret cabal within the CIA threatens to take over the Middle East. In *North by Northwest*, Vandamm is selling government secrets to "the other side." Even in *Alien*, the monster is brought aboard against policy because of surreptitious instructions from the company to the non-human Science Officer Ash. In *Breakdown*, Red and his cronies will continue to bushwhack innocent travelers unless stopped by Jeff Taylor.

108

WRESTLING WITH THE ALTERED REALITY

The menace, then, of each Thriller expands beyond the characters on screen to disturb the sense of security in the audience itself. For a Thriller to be truly successful, the audience must leave the theater slightly on edge, wary, and somewhat more suspicious of the world than they were when they entered. In truth, the Thriller must alter the reality of the audience as well as the characters on screen. Although Thrillers are often thought of as plot-intensive dramas because they are such tightly contrived stories, when they fail to make the audience uneasy, the disappointment is almost always due to botched character set-up.

One-dimensional characters are particularly toxic in Thrillers. It is not especially difficult to set up an intriguing Thriller hook that poses the *What's going to happen?* question to the audience. Far more complex is the issue of *why* something is happening, and the answer to that question is found in the protagonist. Failure to lock in the *why* of the character will inevitably warp the story and cause it to wobble to a flat, unsatisfying conclusion.

This is exactly what occurs in the pseudo-Thriller, *Don't Say a Word*. The film sets up the kidnapping of the main character's child as the driving force for the action. Dr. Nathan Conrad (Michael Douglas) is faced with the same problem that confronts Dr. Ben McKenna (Jimmy Stewart) in *The Man Who Knew Too Much*, Prof. Michael Faraday (Jeff Bridges) in *Arlington Road*, and, for that matter, Tom Mullen (Mel Gibson) in *Ransom*. However, Dr. Conrad is such a one-dimensional character that he is never forced to come to grips with the new reality created by the kidnapping and, therefore, never has to face *himself* in order to save his child.

109

The antagonists in this story exhibit increasingly preposterous abilities to spy on Dr. Conrad's every move, giving them such prescient power that the audience begins to wonder why in the world they need Conrad's help to begin with. But the critical flaw is that Douglas's character never has to stretch, never has to readjust his view of himself. He begins in outrage, and outrage remains the single driving emotion throughout the story until, by miraculous coincidence, he and his daughter are saved by a female police officer who arrives from a wholly separate Narrative Trajectory for the sole purpose of performing the heroics that the lead character should be accomplishing. However, the protagonist is incapable of performing any rescue heroics because he has made no self-discovery. He has literally learned nothing about himself through the ordeal, and therefore returns to his original reality hardly bothered at all by the experience.

How much more impact the story might have had if Dr. Conrad were so imperious that he brags about his ability to extract the secrets of the mind from any patient. Now, when faced with a personal crisis situation, he finds that it is his very self-aggrandizement that has put his daughter in danger, and that his abilities as a psychiatrist are not at all so potent as he has boasted. In the radically altered reality controlled by desperate men who are willing to kill to get their way, Dr. Conrad's own terror as well as the lack of a neatly managed laboratory setting present him with a situation of raw panic that he cannot take charge of so easily. In this new reality, he'd better learn some new skills very fast or both he and his daughter will die.

Similarly, the film *Arlington Road* presents a main character who is already unbalanced, with one foot caught in the quagmire of obsession. Professor Michael Faraday's angry refusal to accept the unjust death of his wife fixes him in the beginning as a character with a mania. It is an awkward position for a Thriller protagonist because Faraday's crucial downfall becomes merely a short tumble instead of the crash-dive plummet that needs to occur to a Thriller protagonist. *Arlington Road* would be a stronger story if the main character were not so emotionally connected to the world of his eventual undoing. If Faraday had no other link than the academic's speculative distance, then the unfolding of the authentic horror in his own neighborhood would be far more devastating to the character, as well as more disturbing to the audience.

BETRAYAL – THE DESTRUCTION OF SELF

In fact, the essence of the Thriller is the irretrievable end of the protagonist's reality. Yet the Thriller protagonist is not one to readily adjust to such a radical change because the character is, in fact, an avoider even of familiar reality. Because of the sudden destruction of the customary world, the Thriller protagonist, like a drowning victim, flails about for salvation, begs for reassurance that the world has not gone off its axis after all. This character who, in one form or another, has avoided personal responsibility, now seeks out that trusted lover, friend, or society that will take on the role of rescuer to lead the return to normalcy.

But it is a critical component of the Thriller film that the main character's plea for help is answered by betrayal, an act that forces the main character to face the unknown dread in the most terrifying human condition possible: being *completely alone*. It is this most primal fear of abandonment that strikes the greatest terror into the character and the audience.

111

Without the forced isolation of betrayal, the protagonist will never be made to face internal inadequacies which must be overcome in order to escape death. The antagonist has no such Achilles' heel. To be sure, there may be intellectual blind spots and strategic chinks in the antagonist's armor, but the protagonist will be unable to recognize these opportunities without first abandoning the unrealistic reliance on someone else for comfort and protection. In other words, the Thriller protagonist must grow up and take charge of life.

The Glass House is a Thriller that is based entirely on the common childhood nightmare of being abandoned by one's parents. In this case the betrayal is the result of death, and the children's whole world is suddenly replaced by an ominous new household that is run by evil guardians. The initial act of betrayal is committed when Ruby (Leelee Sobieski) and Rhett (Trevor Morgan) Baker's parents are killed in a car accident on their way home from an evening out to celebrate their 20th wedding anniversary. Such an unexpected loss naturally has the same impact as deliberate abandonment in the mind of a child. When Ruby and her little brother are sent to live with their guardians, Terry (Stellan Skarsgrd) and Erin (Diane Lane) Glass, they gradually discover an even worse betrayal — the trusted family friends not only have much less than their best interests at heart, but are actually the murderers of their parents. Faced with incontrovertible evidence, Ruby has to take it upon herself to save her vulnerable little brother and expose the Glasses to an incredulous adult world. The modern-day *Hansel and Gretel* story clearly works best for an audience of young people, but it also demonstrates the fundamental childhood fear of raw helplessness that treachery lays bare for the protagonist of any Thriller.

Betrayal within the family is also the impetus for *Single White Female*, as Allie's fiancé, Sam (Steven Weber), cheats on her with another woman. Unable to adjust to the destruction of her reality, Allie throws Sam out of their apartment, which forces her to find a new roommate who can fill the now vacant space. But Allie is not only trying to fill the vacant physical and economic space, she is, unsuspectingly, attempting to recover her reality by stuffing a substitute into the void left by Sam's departure. In her susceptibility, Allie sets herself up for a far worse betrayal. The more she relies on her sympathetic bosom buddy for friendship, the more she fails to accept the ongoing duplicity of the ingenuous Hedy. Only when Allie is forced to adjust her perceptions of Hedy is she also forced to finally take charge of her life — or lose it altogether.

Betrayal can also take on the form of disillusionment. No less devastating than the disloyalty of a loved one, and in some ways more demoralizing, the failure of a trusted institution or an ideal gone wrong can leave the main character so bewildered that even life-saving action is impeded. As mentioned earlier, Joe Turner is the only employee of an obscure CIA auxiliary department to escape assassination in *3 Days of the Condor*. He desperately wants to be safe, to come in off the streets, but he's not sure who to trust. In an arrangement made by the Deputy Director, Turner agrees to meet a CIA contact, Wicks, together with his friend, Sam Barber, in a back alley.

```
TURNER

He takes a breath, moves away from the fire-
exit. He stops in shadows, peers around
corner into the alley.
```

TURNER'S POV

There's Sam Barber, standing against the wall.

TURNER

Relief. He starts around the corner.

ALLEY

Wicks shifts position slightly. Then, suddenly, Wicks deliberately kicks the bottom crate out from under an unsteady stack... the crates crash across the alley.

TURNER

Jumps to one side... reaches toward his gun. Wicks steps quickly out of the shadows now — brings up the silenced Magnum and — incredibly! — fires!

An inch over Turner's head a brick is shattered, sprays down on him... and the ricochet screams.

> BARBER
> (screams)
> <u>Hey!</u> It's him! What're y'doing??!

Turner dives forward and to one side, crashing against garbage cans.

Wicks is unbelievably firing at Turner
<u>again.</u> Turner rolls over the garbage cans,
pulls the gun free. Thrusts it forward in
both hands and pulls the trigger! The Echo
hammers at the walls of the alley. Re-Echo!
Wicks' leg is knocked from under him. He
falls, his thigh shattered.

TURNER

scrambles up, can't believe it.

WICKS

trying to get into position to fire again!

                    TURNER
          Sam??!!

Another round slams past his ear. He runs.

WICKS

on his face, manages to fire again. Then —
he swings his pistol through a quick 90-
degree arc, aims it across the alley —

BARBER

rooted, hypnotized! The stifled sound of
the silenced Magnum! A slug rips through
Barber's throat just above his flak-jacket.

```
EXT.   WEST 74TH STREET & BROADWAY
```

```
Turner, terrified! -- as he bolts out of the
alley...
```

There is no mistake now. Turner is marked for death by the very institution that he trusts. The same people he has counted on for salvation have blown apart Turner's reliance on familiar reality.

THE RETRIEVAL OF LIFE

More than with most other genres, the protagonist of the Thriller is a *relatively* fragile character who has spent life avoiding conflict. In *Executive Decision*, for example, Dr. David Grant (Kurt Russell) is accused by Colonel Austin Travis (Steven Seagal) of having no connection to the blood-and-guts of the military missions he offhandedly plots on paper.

```
                    COL. TRAVIS
          I've read the brief, you did
          consider other — more realistic
          options.

                    GRANT
          Abduction and assassination were
          dismissed early on as too
          inflammatory and dangerous.

                    COL. TRAVIS
          And look at the shit-pot you're in
          now. The Israelis played you like a
```

fish. Only one way to deal with
animals like Jaffa — make them go
away. Pop. Right in the street.
In the back alleys where they live.
The only justice they understand.

        GRANT
State-sanctioned murder is another
form of terrorism, Colonel.

        COL. TRAVIS
Bullshit. Tell that one to the
families who had their children
gunned down in Spain last summer.
You need to come down from that
ivory tower you live in, Grant,
take a look at the real world.
Scum like Jaffa who target women
and children should be treated
like the animals they are.

The protagonist may, of course, have any number of skills valuable in the *former* reality, but the character is at risk when life's positions radically change, as they do for Jeff Taylor (Kurt Russell) in *Breakdown*.

        EARL
You gotta be the dumbest mother-
fucker yet. You think we just
picked you out of the blue?

117

```
New car, Massachusetts plates —
probably be days before anyone
misses you.  Hell, you shoulda got
the bumpersticker that goes with
it: "Rich Assholes Looking for
Trouble!"
```

These dependent, vulnerable protagonists are essential to a successful Thriller Narrative Trajectory because it is only through the absolute destruction of their relatively naive realities that the characters are forced to confront themselves and thereby gain the strength to engage the evil of the antagonist. In other words, they must give up their innocence and come to grips with the brutal world that they have been thrust into in order to save their lives.

LIFE SHRINKS OR EXPANDS IN PROPORTION TO ONE'S COURAGE.

– Anais Nin

In life-threatening ordeals such as drowning, the body reacts to the immediate moment and the primitive brainstem takes over behavioral control of respiration, heart rate, and muscle control to keep the organism functioning. Unfortunately, enduring the immediate moment is not always the best course for staying alive, so Coast Guard rescue swimmers, police and military personnel, and other emergency professionals are trained to counteract the body's intuitive flight-or-fight response, restore the brain's analytical cortex to supremacy, and *think* their way out of hazardous situations.

Having everyday reality ripped away, the only means the unequipped Thriller main character has to regain sanity is through the admission that the old, sentimental, nostalgic vision is no longer valid. Now, like the rescue swimmer plunged into icy water, the character must refuse to yield to instinctual fear, and force intellect to realign perception in order to remain alive. No matter how hopeless the situation, the character has to fight back *alone* because there is no other way to survive.

THE EXPOSURE OF EVIL

Most Thriller films tend to be driven initially by a frantic pursuit that inexorably tightens until the protagonist recognizes that it is impossible to run fast enough or far enough to escape the murderous intent of the antagonist. It is at this stage that the Thriller story takes on the aspect of a State of Siege as the protagonist becomes a kind of detective. The main character must turn and fight, but if the protagonist does not possess martial skills, then whatever tools are at hand will have to do, and that means turning the intellectual tables on the antagonist. In order to win against the antagonist, the character must gather incriminating information that strikes at the antagonist's vulnerability, as Joe Turner does in 3 *Days of the Condor*; outthink the menace, as Ripley (Sigourney Weaver) must in *Alien*; or out-maneuver him as the blind Suzy Hendrix (Audrey Hepburn) does in *Wait Until Dark*, by using the darkness of the apartment to her advantage against the sadistic Harry Roat (Alan Arkin).

THE ALTERED WORLD

Having undergone the extreme trials of the Thriller, the protagonist's Narrative Trajectory comes to earth in new

WRITING THE THRILLER FILM / Hicks

territory that the character must negotiate as a vastly changed person who is now committed to self-sufficiency. It is impossible to return to the complacency of the old way of life. The main character must refuse to remain a victim of the altered reality. In *Breakdown*, Jeff Taylor is pushed to the point of reacting with primitive ferocity.

Red notices his audience is no longer paying
attention. He turns in his chair, sees —

JEFF

Standing in the doorway. Aiming the pistol.
His clothes are caked with blood and dirt.
He sways slightly.

Nobody else moves.

                JEFF
      Give me the key.

                RED
          (placating)
      Now hold on, mister. I don't know
      who you are or what you want —

                JEFF
      <u>GIVE ME THE FUCKING KEY!</u>

There is silence.

120

                    RED
Mister —

                    JEFF
DON'T MISTER ME, YOU SONOFABITCH!
MY WIFE IS LOCKED IN A HOLE IN YOUR
FUCKING BARN!   YOU DON'T GIVE ME
THE KEY, I'LL BLOW YOUR FUCKING
HEAD OFF!

CHAPTER 8

THE FAMILY PLOT

THE THRILLER BLOODLINE

The margins that define the cells of the Genre Continuum are like mesh filters that can allow some of a genre's elements to suffuse from one cell to another. Certain elements, slightly modified as they pass from one story form to the next, may indeed migrate the entire length of the Continuum, so that there's nothing to prohibit the ubiquitous Action-Adventure car chase from making an appearance in the otherwise staid surroundings of the Pivotal Conflict drama.

Assume, for example, that two adult sisters who haven't spoken to each other in years are forced into proximity because of the grave illness and imminent death of their mother. This is, in fact, a characteristic state of affairs for the Pivotal Conflict, one-room dramas of stage and film. In theatre, the playwright can manage the intensity of emotion by sending one or both characters off-stage to help build to a crescendo. The screenwriter, though, looks for movement, even in these most static of dramas, so it would not be unusual for one of the sisters to roar off in her car in an angry, drunken flare of temper. Through regret, concern, or equal hot-headedness, the second sister can burn rubber in a chase after her sibling through the streets. If this action is managed by a skilful screenwriter, the car chase becomes a metaphor for the characters' violent internal frustration. Nevertheless, the inclusion of a surface element normally associated with the Action-Adventure genre does not in any sense make this drama an Action-Adventure.

Similarly, the achievement of self-realization is not limited to those stories where the characters' main goal is to become more fully alive. The need to stay biologically functioning carries with it an inherent dramatic requirement of self-discovery. The story of life is, in fact, about the struggle to know ourselves. Dramatic stories, however, put immediate and massive pressure on characters to achieve that knowledge under extraordinary circumstances. As discussed in *Screenwriting 101: The Essential Craft Of Feature Film Writing*, the protagonist in a drama is always, in one respect, also the antagonist. That is, in order to do battle against the personified opposition, the main character must first come to grips with the heretofore ignored internal need. A good Thriller story, then, is satisfying to the audience not merely because the main character escapes death or puts a stop to the malevolence of the antagonist, but because in achieving these ends the character is required by the pressures of the story to grow — to overcome the terror within.

So there are not only certain surface level actions that may appear in different film genres, but also core requisites of drama that function in all stories. Like birds building their nests, genres borrow bits of string, twigs, and the occasional bright bauble to structure environments for their stories. At first glance, all these nests may look alike, but a close examination reveals the subtleties of architecture that distinguish one species of inhabitants from another.

As observed earlier, the Thriller is an extremely difficult genre to write because of the aesthetic demand that the story *seem* to be unquestionably real while at the same time it is the most contrived and artificial of all dramas. This incongruity is more perplexing because the borrowings that make up the Thriller habitat are taken from both the most rational and intellectually rigorous genre, as well as from the most speculative, emotional, and least scrupulous — the Detective and Horror film genres.

YOU'RE SUPPOSED TO *DO* SOMETHING.
   – Sam Spade, *The Maltese Falcon*

The classic movie detectives, of course, are the hard-boiled creations of authors Raymond Chandler and Dashiell Hammett, and the hundreds of B-Movie tough guys that their characters spawned, not to mention the archetypal investigators of the Agatha Christie variety. However, Detective films do not necessarily require the cynical shamus or the world-weary cop. The job of a movie detective is to search for truth, in which capacity the character may be a doctor, an attorney, a scientist, or a factory worker who comes to grips with some overarching risk to society.

The Andromeda Strain and *Contact* each cast scientists in the role of detective. In *The Sixth Sense* it's a psychiatrist; in *The Verdict*, an attorney. *Silkwood* and *Erin Brockovich* are outraged crusaders, and the intrigue of *The China Syndrome* catches up a TV reporter. Naturally, Detective films are still patrolled by real screen cops as well. *The Silence of the Lambs* scatters the board with the baffling clues of one psychopath to catch another. *L.A. Confidential* is a pulp crime snarl of corruption. *Chinatown* descends into the incestuous slough of Los Angeles.

What all these Detective protagonists have in common with each other, unlike their Action-Adventure counterparts, is that they are characters possessed of intellect over physical strength. They are thinkers who must coax answers from enigmatic schemes rather than blast their way through them. Of course, they may at some point or another have to use physical force, but the fierce confrontations of Action-Adventure are beyond the scope of the Detective story. Instead, the Detective genre is the most cerebral of film stories, challenging the audience to solve the mystery along with the detective.

The Thriller inherits this analytical approach to a predicament from the Detective genre. The Thriller protagonist must outwit the opposition because there is no way to overpower it. There is, however, a subtle but crucial difference between the Detective and the Thriller characters who are engaged in their puzzles.

Like the Action-Adventure protagonist, the Detective protagonist willingly enters the conflict and is, at least to some degree, prepared to meet the opposition head-on. And, like the Action-Adventure protagonists, the Detective hero possesses an official sanction of some nature: a doctor, a lawyer, a cop, or a private eye who has been legally constituted to engage the fight. More important, the detective is equipped with a moral imperative, an inviolable code of honor, that provides the audience's deputization to act.

Conversely, the Thriller protagonist is hurled unwilling into the fray and is therefore neither equipped by temperament or by moral stance to take on the fight. The character's own lack of commitment must be overcome in order to *earn* the right to act on behalf of society.

The Detective story is not about defeating all evil for all time, or even about justice, but about the restoration of equilibrium. It

126

is a polluted, distasteful business dealing with the soft underbelly of civilization, but society has developed a malignant aneurysm and the detective's job is to clamp the abscess before it bursts into the world at large. The Thriller protagonist, on the other hand, becomes the lone outrider protecting the unguarded flank of the societal body from an exterior menace. The threat posed by the Thriller antagonist is most often an ominous treachery that would succeed if it were not for the inadvertent hindrance of the Thriller protagonist. The *Alien* monster would be returned to earth by the unscrupulous company. The secret cabal within the CIA would succeed in *3 Days of the Condor*. It is only through the intervention of the Thriller main character that the deceitful treason is brought into the open.

It is also true that the *crucial* Narrative Trajectory of a Detective film is not concerned with the life or the death of the detective. Of course, the detective's life may be in jeopardy at any given point in the story to achieve the goal, for instance, of saving someone else's life, but the story is about the solving of the mystery, not about the detective's self-preservation. The Thriller protagonist, however, always acts in self-interest because the Thriller protagonist's specific, individual life is at risk from the inception of the story.

So the Detective and Thriller protagonists each enter their dramas for different reasons, because action must be taken to protect a person or a society from the antagonist, or because self-preservation is imperative. Both protagonists face a powerful evil that threatens the very society in which they live, and in both cases, the protagonists must use intelligence rather than physical strength in order to overcome the opposition. However, the Detective character has access to resources and power of a special authority, whereas the Thriller character lacks not only substantial resources but moral commitment as well. In the process of resolving the Detective story, the main character, in fact, uncovers more questions, including self-doubt about how the character's own actions have contributed to society's vulnerability. The Thriller character's resolution of the dramatic conflict, on the other hand, earns the protagonist a strength of individual commitment that was previously lacking.

IT's ALIVE!

> – Dr. Frankenstein, *Frankenstein*

The contemporary Horror film genre is a direct outgrowth of generations of folklore, fairy tales, and pagan mythologies that have defined the mortal boundaries of the human race in a phantasmagoric universe. Until the Roman Church established its dominance in Europe, the pagan cultures from which the West draws its narrative traditions lived in a polytheistic universe where manifold gods held influence over the affairs of humankind as well as the flow of rivers, the turning of the heavens, and the very ground on which men walked. With the aid of soothsayers, divination, magical amulets, and accumulated folk wisdom, generations of Celts, Picts, Saxons, and dozens of other ancestral cultures negotiated the turmoil of their physical world, and transformed the terrors of the unknown into bodily beings that could be bargained with head-on as mortal-to-manifestation.

The Church, however, replaced the approachable pagan divinities with a distant God of abstractions, leaving the common folk no recourse for the terrors of the mind that formerly were conferred on the malicious spirits of forest, land, and water. Instead, these pagan charismas and their rituals were drafted by the Church into innocuous elves, harmless animals, decorated trees, and childlike holidays, even though the unpredictable horrors of life that beset human kind remained, and the terrors of mind did not cease.

ABANDON ALL HOPE, YOU WHO ENTER!

> – *Inferno*, canto 3.1.1 Dante Alighieri

By the Middle Ages, the poet Dante Alighieri in *The Divine Comedy* and painters like Hieronymus Bosch in *The Garden of Earthly Delights* had replaced the woodland deities with horrendous tortures, carnal mutilations, and the fires of Hell presided over by a single demonic being who could be held responsible for all the ills on earth. Today's Horror genre continues to exploit that same imagery in order to expiate the audience's fears and give them the means to overcome the Devil's dominion.

Because the torments of mankind are universal, the protagonist of the Horror film is most often the same vulnerable *everyman* who is the main character of a Thriller. And, like the Thriller protagonist, the Horror protagonist ordinarily is thrust unwillingly into the battle against evil. However, whereas the Thriller character is drafted into the drama more or less at random, the Horror film protagonist is, like the Detective hero, at least in part responsible for the predicament. The Horror protagonist has *transgressed*, has in some manner broken the rules and therefore unleashed the evil on the world.

Poltergeist flouts the hidden mysteries of the dead by building a housing development on an Indian burial ground. The teenagers frolicking through infinite remakes of *Friday the 13th* continue to trespass in forbidden landscapes of both morality and environment. Renfield's obsequious eagerness to please the

129

Count in *Dracula* makes him the unwitting agent for the rebirth of the undead. The monster of *Frankenstein* is the product of scientific curiosity unbridled by principle, just as the monster Alex in *Fatal Attraction* is the product of unrestrained sexual obsession.

The Horror protagonist, like the Thriller main character and each individual audience member, is tested against these invincible horrors. But here there is an important distinction between the antagonist of the Horror film and that of the Detective or Thriller genre. The opposition in a Horror film is *inhuman*. Whether the monster is a grotesque beast or a camouflaged fiend that masquerades as human, the antagonist is empowered by a supernatural Satanic legacy. Yet, if the antagonist is truly immortal, then there is no way for the protagonist to win, no way for the audience to overcome fear. The antagonist must, therefore, have a vulnerability that the protagonist can exploit. It is not for nothing that vampires fear daylight, wooden stakes, mirrors, and crucifixes. Without such tools, mankind would be at the mercy of the Devil's minions.

The Narrative Trajectory of a Horror film, then, has to do with raw fear. The terror of a supernatural monster that has absolute power over its human victims is expressed, not in suspense like the Thriller, but in repeated shocks as the protagonist pursues the antagonist through a world that is isolated from any outside help, a distorted maze of corridors and unknown recesses from which the monster can emerge at any moment. In the end, however, man's resourcefulness proves the undoing of the beast. Through courage and perseverance, human faith and ingenuity triumph over supernatural chaos. The world is returned to order; the Devil contained once again in his realm.

GENRE GENEOLOGY

The following diagram illustrates that the immediate Detective and Horror forebears of the Thriller on the Genre Continuum contribute more to its pedigree than it passes along to its Action-Adventure successor.

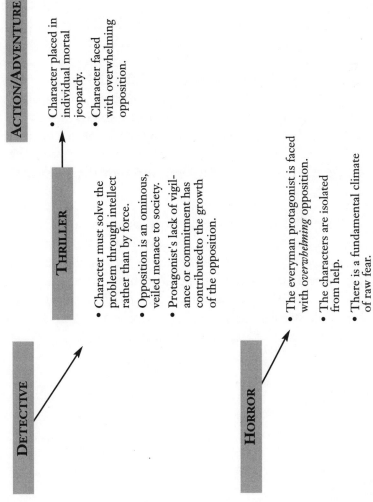

ACTION/ADVENTURE
- Character placed in individual mortal jeopardy.
- Character faced with overwhelming opposition.

THRILLER
- Character must solve the problem through intellect rather than by force.
- Opposition is an ominous, veiled menace to society.
- Protagonist's lack of vigilance or commitment has contributed to the growth of the opposition.

HORROR
- The everyman protagonist is faced with *overwhelming* opposition.
- The characters are isolated from help.
- There is a fundamental climate of raw fear.

DETECTIVE

A SHIVER OF PERIPHERAL INSTINCT. SOMETHING IS NOT QUITE KNOWN.

So why is it that so many contemporary movies frequently bowdlerize the Thriller into a misshapen Action-Adventure? No doubt a good part of the answer lies with the delusions of studios, stars, marketing, and money. Even more at fault is the uncertainty of semantics. Critics, reviewers, and the media publicity machine refer to a film such as *Insomnia* as a Thriller. However, the film is unquestionably a Detective story about an armed, professional police officer with a duty to track down a killer. It is stylish, well-directed, and tightly written, but except for the fact that there is some suspense contained within individual scenes, it has virtually nothing in common with a true Thriller. What the story does involve that should be an integral part of all Thrillers is an inherent weakness in the main character that must be overcome through the pressures of the drama.

Most so-called Thrillers fall short as representatives of their genre because the protagonist's core seems to exist outside the reach of the action, and therefore no self-examination can take place. The result is that even those films which begin with an engaging Thriller premise, such as *The Panic Room*, ultimately generate suspense only through anxious music and *camera-bravura* spectacle in place of substance.

THE POWERS OF EVIL ARE TOO GREAT FOR THOSE WITH WEAK MINDS.

– Renfield, *Dracula*

It is not that we lack the stuff for movies to be about, but perhaps as screenwriters and studio executives we lack the heart to chronicle the evils of our time. It is easier to fashion antagonists of straw and charades of action than it is to take on the furtive villainy in the world. The chronic psychopath-in-ski-mask is an icon that requires no effort on the part of the writer or the audience. But such a character also lacks the ominous chill of genuinely shrewd wickedness. At worst, such antagonists exhibit a callous sadism that is not supported by any philosophical allegiance. Short of being mean and nasty for the sake of being mean and nasty, they are devoid of a point of view that compels the protagonist to reinterpret life.

In other words, these counterfeit Thrillers are not *about* anything. If a Thriller does not cause the audience to steal an extra glance over the shoulder, then the film has not disjointed the reality outside the theater. A good Thriller is founded on an ill-omened, pervasive menace, but if the screenwriter abdicates the responsibility for creating that shiver of doubt in the main character, the resonance of fear will not alter everyday life.

What is a Dickian Friendship?
- Detached acceptance.
- Open to each other's craziness.
- The Dickian Friend has few
  assumptions, they are young
  at heart. This is connected
  to hallucinogen use.
- Open to adventure.
- First person spirituality. No respect
  for convention.
- Lack of materialism
- They are not naive.

This could be why
134 Hollywood chooses
to adopt his →
short fiction; The Dickian
Friendship is not fleshed out.

CHAPTER 9

THE QUINTESSENTIAL THRILLER

No movie genre exists in its purest form any more than a novel, painting, dance, or symphony. The hypothetical, conjectural, and paradigmatic models we construct can never take into account all the variables inherent in the real world of creation. When a screenwriter's fingers hover over the keyboard, it is not with visions of speculative theories tracing a framework on the screen.

Nevertheless, if it is possible to express the Thriller Narrative Trajectory at its simplest, the classic story would be:

THE CLASSIC THRILLER

A relatively innocent character who normally avoids commitment and dissociates from conflict in life is abruptly caught in the snare of a menacing conspiracy.

The character is completely bewildered and wants nothing more than to return to the normalcy of everyday life, but a powerful antagonist is committed to killing the main character in order to achieve a goal that threatens not only the protagonist, but the community at large.

The protagonist, spurred by uncontrollable panic, runs to escape the antagonist, yet soon discovers that not only is escape impossible, but that there is no help forthcoming from supposed friends or trusted institutions.

Instead, the protagonist must act alone by acquiring the strength of self-sufficiency and out-maneuvering the antagonist in a battle of wits until, in the final confrontation, the protagonist defeats the menace by attacking the antagonist's vulnerability and exposing the evil.

Having changed from an avoider of conflict to a self-sufficient person, the protagonist now must face the larger world with a keenly sharpened vigilance.

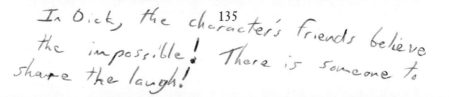

In Dick, the character's friends believe the impossible! There is someone to share the laugh!

The obvious danger in compacting the essence of the Thriller genre into such a statement is that it appears to be a formula. This Classic Thriller story is no recipe, however, but a condensation of all the essential elements that make the Thriller genre what it is.

Although there may be no single Thriller film that precisely fits the prototype, Ernest Lehman's screenplay for *North by Northwest* is about as faultless an example of any genre as possible. In fact, it can be argued that *North by Northwest* is possibly the most perfectly structured screen story of any genre ever written.

The actual genesis of the film is intriguing because, like many of Alfred Hitchcock's works, it began as nothing more substantial than a single-scene mental image from the director: "You know, I've always wanted to do a chase across the faces of Mount Rushmore."[19] While Alfred Hitchcock receives ample praise as a unique director of the Thriller form, such a modest beginning for *North by Northwest* bears out the genius of Ernest Lehman as a screenwriter. Yet even a cursory glance at Lehman's screenplay will reveal that it is written in a style that would be completely out of place today. It contains large, unbroken blocks of text that are nearly word-for-word descriptive of the action on the screen.

Today's screenplays tend to be written in less literal, although equally expressive descriptions. Ernest Lehman, though, like William Goldman, came to screenwriting from the profession of fiction writing, and he was working hand-in-glove with Hitchcock, so much of his writing arose from detailed discussions with the director.

---

[19] Ernest Lehman, "How the Hell Should I Know? Tales from My Anecdotage," *Written By, The Magazine of the Writers Guild of America*, Vol.5, #6, (June/July, 2001).

Likewise, although the actual movie of *North by Northwest* is thoroughly engaging as a genuine classic almost fifty years after its creation, there are, inescapably, some characteristics that may seem quaint to today's viewers. Aside from dated production values such as rear-screen projections, there is an overall manner of polished urbanity that would doubtless seem out of place if the film were made now. However, it must be remembered that Alfred Hitchcock was not merely a talented director, he was unconditionally a studio director. Hitch was acutely mindful of casting his pictures with the studio's top-of-the-line talent, which often meant tailoring the film to fit the persona of the star. The drawing power of *North by Northwest* star Cary Grant was a unique, carefully cultivated screen personality that audiences came to see regardless of the story. So certain scenes in the film are unquestionably in place for Cary Grant to do Cary Grant.

To the credit of Ernest Lehman as a brilliant writer, though, even those set-piece scenes carry essential plot information. In fact, what makes the screenplay for *North by Northwest* not only the quintessential Thriller, but one of the best screenplays ever written, is that virtually every scene contains new information which inevitably drives the plot forward. Lehman constructs the labyrinth of fear block by block, and consequently steers the main character into a confrontation not only with the antagonist but with himself — a clash that is an essential hallmark of the Thriller.

By following the plot outline below while watching the film several times, it is possible to learn a great deal about this unique genre we call the Thriller.

137

Story Outline for
NORTH BY NORTHWEST
by
Ernest Lehman

Act I

Midtown Manhattan, the tempo of Madison Avenue, streets swarming with smartly dressed people. V.O. "Would it not be strange, in a city of seven million people, if one man were <u>never</u> mistaken for another..."

ROGER THORNHILL, tall, lean, faultlessly dressed, and far too original to be wearing the gray flannel uniform of his kind. Thornhill is effete, not altogether serious about life, and very uncommitted.

Thornhill meets business associates for lunch. When he excuses himself from the table to go send a telegram to his mother, LICHT and VALERIAN assume that he is "George Kaplan." They hustle him into a waiting car at gunpoint, refusing to tell him why he's being taken or where.

Thornhill is delivered to the Townsend estate on Long Island, where he meets a MAN (PHILLIP VANDAMM) who also believes Thornhill is the someone named George Kaplan. Vandamm accuses Thornhill of lying, and questions him on how much he knows about "our arrangements." When Thornhill denies knowing anything, Vandamm's personal assistant LEONARD, along with Valerian and Licht, hold Thornhill down and pour a fifth of bourbon into him.

Act I (Con't)

Valerian and Licht put a thoroughly drunk Thornhill behind the wheel of a car and set it moving on a winding mountain road. Thornhill manages to steer the car until he is intercepted by a police cruiser and arrested. Valerian and Licht sneak away unnoticed.

Thornhill, his mother, his lawyer, and two cops all return to the Townsend mansion to verify his fantastic story. A WOMAN who appears to be Mrs. Townsend tells the officers that Thornhill attended a party the night before and drove away drunk. She says that her husband is addressing the United Nations today. But as Thornhill and the others leave, they are watched suspiciously by a gardener (Valerian).

Thornhill and his mother finagle their way into George Kaplan's room at the Plaza Hotel. The hotel staff also assumes that Thornhill is Kaplan because they have never actually seen Mr. Kaplan in person. Thornhill discovers a newspaper clipping picture of the man "Townsend" from the Long Island house.

Thornhill goes to the United Nations. Pretending to be George Kaplan, he requests a meeting with Townsend. However, when Mr. Townsend appears, he is not at all the same man from the mansion. As Valerian watches them from the background, Thornhill shows Townsend the newspaper photo. Townsend suddenly gasps — then falls into Thornhill with a knife in his back. Thornhill grabs for him, and his picture holding the knife above the dead man is snapped by a newspaper photographer.

Act II

A group of CIA bureaucrats are looking at the same photograph of Thornhill holding the knife on the front page of the newspaper. They regret that Thornhill has been mistaken for the nonexistent George Kaplan but, "There's nothing we can do to save him without endangering Number One!"

Thornhill boards a train for Chicago. He eludes the police with the help of EVE KENDALL, who hides him in her sleeping compartment. But Eve sends a note via the porter to PHILLIP VANDAMM: "What do I do with him in the morning?"

In Chicago, Eve arranges for Thornhill to meet "Kaplan." The rendezvous is in a rural corn field, where Thornhill is attacked by a crop duster plane. He survives the attack and returns to find Eve getting ready to meet Vandamm. He follows them to an art auction where Vandamm is picking up a statue filled with microfilm. Thornhill confronts Vandamm. Leonard and Valerian prevent Thornhill's escape, but he causes a commotion and is arrested by the police.

In the police car, Thornhill confesses that he is a wanted murderer. But instead of taking him to jail, the police deliver him to the airport, where he is met by the PROFESSOR, the head of the CIA group.

Thornhill learns that Vandamm is an international smuggler of secrets, that Eve is actually a CIA agent, and his love affair with her has endangered her life.

Act II (Con't)

To convince Vandamm that Kaplan is no longer a threat and that Eve is loyal, the Professor stages Thornhill's death at Mt. Rushmore by having Eve shoot him with blanks.

Act III

Thornhill and Eve meet after the shooting. They confess their love for each other — but Eve is leaving the country with Vandamm that night, and will never return. Thornhill tries to stop her but the Professor has him knocked unconscious. Eve leaves to join Vandamm.

Thornhill escapes the Professor's protective custody and goes to Vandamm's house to keep Eve from leaving. He discovers that Leonard and Vandamm know she's a spy and intend to kill her.

Thornhill manages to get Eve and the statue containing the microfilm away from Vandamm and Leonard. They are pursued on foot through the woods until they emerge on the top of Mt. Rushmore.

Trying to climb down the treacherous slope, they are attacked by Valerian and Leonard until the Professor's sharpshooter kills Leonard. Thornhill strains to rescue Eve from where she has fallen, pulling her up until —

— "Mrs. Thornhill" lands beside him in the upper berth of a drawing room on a train, and the two of them speed off into the night.

141

EPILOGUE

duckspeak — To speak without thinking.
– George Orwell, *Newspeak Dictionary*

The immobilizing confusion of fear impacts not only individuals, as expressed in a Thriller film, but often whole societies. We have only to look into the faces of the refugees driven from Bosnia, Afghanistan, Goma, and a hundred other places on the globe spiked with the violence of war or the upheavals of nature to see the radical change wrought with brusque indifference upon mankind's reality.

When it comes to terror, we are creatures no different from gazelles, alligators, grizzly bears, or pussycats. It does not matter in the least if the threat that causes our fear is innate or learned [19], the brain's amygdala that controls defensive responses reacts exactly the same way.

As a result, animals and humans alike are condemned to repeat the experience of fear endlessly, whether threatened by the pounce of a hungry predator, the nocturnal tiptoe of a downstairs burglar, the memory of a mother's reproving voice, or the recurrent vision of terrorist atrocity. They're all the same to the amygdala, which immediately doses the body with put-up-your-dukes or get-the-hell-outa-town juices in a life-saving response which, for the most part, impudently slams the door on the brain's rational cortex altogether.

---

[19] Joseph Le Doux, *Synaptic Self: How Our Brains become Who We Are*, (Viking Press, 2002).

Humans, though, have evolved a singular advantage over the other primates with whom we share this inescapable torment: We can *talk* about it. We can describe our fears and tell *stories* to put those fears in their place. It is the human facility with language that allows us to rewrite our reality, to fine-tune ourselves through the art of narrative. As individuals we recount a traumatic experience until it fits manageably within the scheme of our life. If we fail to do so, the emotional shock of random fright can so overwhelm our senses that it becomes confused with other doubts and vulnerabilities and makes those frailties far more dreadful than they should otherwise be.

Likewise, as a society we are subject to the same risk that overpowering fear may devastate our cultural self. The terrorist attack on the World Trade Center has made the *ethos* of the American people vulnerable as never before.[20] In our heedless rush to reconstitute reality, we have allowed the national limbic system to run rampant until there is a danger of reducing the societal consciousness to such inexact concepts as color-coded alerts, and the ubiquitous admonitions to remain *on guard*. Such vague imprecations are, like Orwell's Newspeak[21], language that limits the range of ideas that can be expressed and the literary value of writing until clarity of thought is nearly abolished.

Since the guardian monks of Ireland salvaged the written word from the ravages of the Dark Ages, writers have been the practitioners of clarity of thought. We live in times no less perilous now for the richness of language. Yet, these are also times that are intense with the need for stories, and therefore incumbent on all those who call themselves wordsmiths not to succumb to the imprecision of fuzzy philosophies of duckspeak.

---

[20] e.g, "Bracing for Trauma's Second Wave," *The Wall Street Journal*, March 5, 2002.

[21] George Orwell, *Nineteen Eighty-Four*, (ISBN: 0451 524 934 1949 Harcourt Brace Javanovich, Inc.)

Like the protagonist of a Thriller, our only salvation is to wrench ourselves into deliberate control of the new reality, for it is only through the conscientious use of language that writers will be able to create the significant stories that can overcome fear and restore authenticity to the national experience.

REFERENCED FILMS

FILM TITLE	YEAR	SCREENWRITER(S)	DIRECTOR(S)
African Queen, The	1951	James Agee and John Huston from the C. S. Forester novel	John Huston
Alien	1979	Dan O'Bannon	Ridley Scott
Aliens	1986	James Cameron from the James Cameron and David Giler and Walter Hill story	James Cameron
Andromeda Strain, The	1971	Michael Crichton, Nelson Gidding from the Michael Crichton novel	Robert Wise
Arlington Road	1999	Ehren Kruger	Mark Pellington
Basic Instinct	1992	Joe Eszterhas	Paul Verhoeven
Beautiful Mind, A	2001	Akiva Goldsman from the Sylvia Nasar book	Ron Howard
Ben-Hur	1959	Karl Tunberg from the Lew Wallace novel	William Wyler
Breakdown	1997	Jonathan Mostow and Sam Montgomery from the Jonathan Mostow story	Jonathan Mostow
Casablanca	1942	Julius J. Epstein and Philip G. Epstein and Howard Koch from the Murray Burnett and Joan Alison play	Michael Curtiz
China Syndrome, The	1979	Mike Gray & T.S. Cook and James Bridges	James Bridges
Chinatown	1974	Robert Towne	Roman Polanski
Contact	1997	James V. Hart and Michael Goldenberg from the Carl Sagan novel and the Carl Sagan and Ann Druyan story	Robert Zemeckis
Copycat	1995	Ann Biderman and David Madsen	Jon Amiel
Dead Man Walking	1995	Tim Robbins from the Helen Prejean book	Tim Robbins
Don't Say a Word	2001	Anthony Peckham and Patrick Smith Kelly from the Andrew Klavan novel	Gary Fleder

Dracula	*1931*	*John L. Balderston, Hamilton Deane, Garret Ford from the Balderston and Dean play and the Bram Stoker novel*	*Tod Browning*
Enemy of the State	*1998*	*David Marconi*	*Tony Scott*
Erin Brockovich	*2000*	*Susannah Grant*	*Steven Soderbergh*
Executive Decision	*1996*	*Jim Thomas & John Thomas*	*Stuart Baird*
Fatal Attraction	*1987*	*James Dearden, Nicholas Meyer*	*Adrian Lyne*
Frankenstein	*1931*	*John L. Balderston, Francis Edward Faragoh & Garrett Fort from the Peggy Webling play and the Mary Shelley novel*	*James Whale*
Friday the 13th	*1980*	*Victor Miller; Sean S. Cunningham*	*Sean S. Cunningham*
Gladiator	*2000*	*David Franzoni and John Logan and William Nicholson*	*Ridley Scott*
Glass House, The	*2001*	*Wesley Strick*	*Daniel Sackheim*
Good Will Hunting	*1997*	*Matt Damon & Ben Affleck*	*Gus Van Sant*
Halloween	*1978*	*John Carpenter and Debra Hill*	*John Carpenter*
Insomnia	*2002*	*Hillary Seitz from the Nikolaj Frobenius and Erik Skoldbjerg screenplay*	*Christopher Nolan*
Into the Night	*1985*	*Ron Koslow*	*John Landis*
Jaws	*1975*	*Peter Benchley & Carl Gottlieb from the Peter Benchley novel*	*Steven Spielberg*
L.A. Confidential	*1997*	*Brian Helgeland & Curtis Hanson from the James Ellroy novel*	*Curtis Hanson*
Maltese Falcon, The	*1941*	*John Huston from the Dashiell Hammett novel*	*John Huston*
Man Who Knew Too Much, The	*1956*	*John Michael Hayes from the Charles Bennett and D. B. Wyndham-Lewis story*	*Alfred Hitchcock*
Marathon Man	*1976*	*William Goldman*	*John Schlesinger*
Matrix, The	*1999*	*The Wachowski Brothers*	*Andy Wachowski Larry Wachowski*

Moulin Rouge!	2001	Baz Luhrmann & Craig Pearce	Baz Luhrmann
North by Northwest	1957	Ernest Lehman	Alfred Hitchcock
Panic Room, The	2002	David Koepp	David Fincher
Poltergeist	1982	Steven Spielberg & Michael Grais & Mark Victor from the Steven Spielberg story	Tobe Hooper
Pretty Woman	1990	J.F. Lawton	Garry Marshall
Psycho	1960	Joe Stefano from the Robert Bloch novel	Alfred Hitchcock
Quiz Show	1994	Paul Attanasio from the Richard N. Goodwin book	Robert Redford
Ransom	1996	Richard Price and Alexander Ignon from the Cyril Hume and Richard Maibaum story	Ron Howard
Rebel Without a Cause	1955	Stewart Stern	Nicholas Ray
Shane	1953	A.B. Guthrie from the Jack Schaefer story	George Stevens
Silence of the Lambs, The	1991	Ted Tally from the Thomas Harris novel	Jonathan Demme
Silkwood	1983	Alice Arlen, Nora Ephron	Mike Nichols
Single White Female	1992	Don Roos from the John Lutz novel	Barbet Schroeder
Sixth Sense, The	1999	M. Night Shyamalan	M. Night Shyamalan
Star Wars	1977	George Lucas	George Lucas
3 Days of the Condor	1975	Lorenzo Semple, Jr. and David Rayfiel from the James Grady novel	Sydney Pollack
Titanic	1997	James Cameron	James Cameron
Usual Suspects, The	1995	Christopher McQuarrie	Bryan Singer
Verdict, The	1982	David Mamet from the Barry Reed novel	Sidney Lumet
Wait Until Dark	1967	Robert Howard-Carrington & Jane Howard-Carrington from the Frederick Knott play	Terence Young

149

NEILL D. HICKS

NEILL D. HICKS is a screenwriter specializing in Thriller and Action-Adventure films such as Pierce Brosnan's *Don't Talk to Strangers* and the critically acclaimed *Dead Reckoning*. At the same time, he has written the screenplays for European and Asian productions, including three Scandinavian films, the animated feature of the epic Indian narrative poem the *Mahabharath*, and two  simultaneous #1 box-office films in the world: Jackie Chan's *Rumble in the Bronx* and *First Strike*. He recently completed the feature story *Ghost Writer* for the Academy Award-winning Italian filmmakers of *Il Postino*. His scripts for *The Anodyne Conduct*, a chilling, near-future political thriller, and *The Misgiven*, a tale of romance and deceit in the cabals of the Dark Ages, are in development in Hollywood.

Neill's initial book, *Screenwriting 101: The Essential Craft Of Feature Film Writing*, has been a worldwide success, particularly as more European and Asian filmmakers search for ways to structure their stories in a global market. His innovative

analysis of the principles of film genre writing continues in two more volumes, *Writing the Action-Adventure Film* and this book, *Writing the Thriller Film*. His consulting services as the acknowledged industry expert on film genres are in demand on both U.S. and international productions. His insight into the meaning that underlies the structure of a screenplay applies to his own writing as well, because he welds plot and character together with a Narrative Trajectory in a way that grabs hold of what the audience instinctively cares about.

With a background in documentary as well as fiction film, Neill has also created diverse programs from WWII's *Operation Pointblank* for A&E's *Masters of War Series*, to the *Children's Crusade* of the 13th Century for The History Channel. His work as a theatrical director has spanned productions from Gilbert and Sullivan's *The Mikado* to Shakespeare's *Taming of the Shrew*. In academia, he has been honored with the Outstanding Instructor Award at the UCLA Extension Writers' Program, and has been a guest lecturer in screenwriting at Northwestern University, the University of Wisconsin, California State University, and the Canadian Television & Film Institute. He is a member of the adjunct faculty of the University of Denver, and an advisor to the Studiesenteret for Film in Oslo, Norway.

SCREENWRITING 101
The Essential Craft of Feature Film Writing

Neill D. Hicks

Hicks brings the clarity and practical instruction familiar to his students and readers to screenwriters everywhere. In his inimitable and colorful style, he tells the beginning screenwriter how the mechanics of Hollywood storytelling work, and how to use those elements to create a script with blockbuster potential without falling into clichés.

$16.95, 220 pages | Order # 41RLS | ISBN: 0-941188-72-8

SCREENWRITING ON THE INTERNET
Researching, Writing and Selling Your Script on the Web

Christopher Wehner

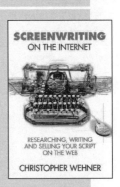

The Internet can save you loads of money, time, and effort — but only if you know how to exploit it. This book is your road map to using the information superhighway to further your screenwriting career. Packed with time- and money-saving tips, it includes a definitive directory and much more.

$16.95, 235 pages | Order # 5RLS | ISBN: 0-941188-36-1

FADE IN:
The Screenwriting Process, 2nd Edition

Robert A. Berman

With this concise step-by-step roadmap for developing a story concept into a finished screenplay, you will learn how to: read a screenplay; analyze a script; create three-dimensional characters; structure your story; structure your screenplay; research effectively; format professionally; use the correct terms and techniques; write the first draft; rewrite and polish until you have a final draft you are proud to submit.

$24.95, 385 Pages | Order # 30RLS | ISBN: 0-941188-58-2

WRITING THE ACTION-ADVENTURE FILM
The Moment of Truth

Neill D. Hicks

The Action-Adventure movie is consistently one of the most popular exports of the American film industry, drawing enormous audiences worldwide across many diverse societies, cultures, and languages.

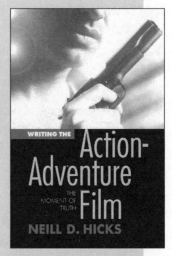

But there are more than hot pursuits, hot lead, and hotheaded slugfests in a successful Action-Adventure script. With definitive examples from over 100 movies, *Writing the Action-Adventure Film* reveals the screenwriting principles that define the content and the style of this popular film genre. Neill Hicks furnishes a set of tools to build a compelling screenplay that fulfills the expectations of the motion picture audience.

You will discover how to create the Moment of Truth where the stakes are life and death, perfect a story structure that compels your characters to take immediate action, recognize the different forms of action and where to use them effectively, and develop the narrative context of adventure to surround the audience in the special world of the story.

"Dreaming about writing the next *The Matrix*, *Gladiator*, *The One*, or *Spy Game*? Neill clearly knows the Action-Adventure genre inside and out. I recommend the book highly!"

> — Eric Lilleør
> Publisher/Editor-in-Chief
> *Screentalk Magazine*

Neill D. Hicks, the author of the best-selling *Screenwriting 101: The Essential Craft of Feature Film Writing* (see page 21) and *Writing the Thriller Film: The Terror Within* (see page 8), is an L.A.-based professional screenwriter whose credits include two of the biggest Action-Adventure films of all time, *Rumble in the Bronx* and *First Strike*.

$14.95, 180 pages
Order # 99RLS
ISBN: 0-941188-39-6

THE WRITER'S JOURNEY
2nd Edition
Mythic Structure for Writers

Christopher Vogler

Over 100,000 units sold!

See why this book has become an international bestseller and a true classic. *The Writer's Journey* explores the powerful relationship between mythology and storytelling in a clear, concise style that's made it required reading for movie executives, screenwriters, playwrights, scholars, and fans of pop culture all over the world.

Both fiction and nonfiction writers will discover a set of useful myth-inspired storytelling paradigms (i.e., "The Hero's Journey") and step-by-step guidelines to plot and character development. Based on the work of Joseph Campbell, *The Writer's Journey* is a must for all writers interested in further developing their craft.

The updated and revised second edition provides new insights and observations from Vogler's ongoing work on mythology's influence on stories, movies, and man himself.

"This book is like having the smartest person in the story meeting come home with you and whisper what to do in your ear as you write a screenplay. Insight for insight, step for step, Chris Vogler takes us through the process of connecting theme to story and making a script come alive."
> — Lynda Obst, Producer
> *Sleepless in Seattle, Contact, Someone Like You*
> Author, *Hello, He Lied*

Christopher Vogler, a top Hollywood story consultant and development executive, has worked on such high-grossing feature films as *The Lion King* and conducts writing workshops around the globe.

$24.95, 325 pages
Order #98RLS
ISBN: 0-941188-70-1

THE SCRIPT-SELLING GAME
A Hollywood Insider's Look at Getting Your Script Sold and Produced

Kathie Fong Yoneda

There are really only two types of people in Hollywood: those who sit around wearing black clothes in smoky coffee shops, complaining they can't get their scripts past the studio gates... and then there are the players. The ones with the hot scripts. The ones crackling with energy. The ones with knowledge.

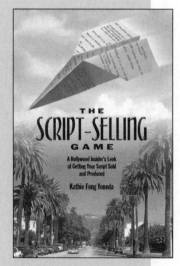

Players understand that their success in Hollywood is not based on luck or nepotism; it's the result of understanding how Hollywood really works.

The Script-Selling Game brings together over 25 years of experience from an entertainment professional who shows you how to prepare your script, pitch it, meet the moguls, talk the talk, and make the deal. It's a must for both novice and veteran screenwriters.

"Super-concise, systematic, real-world advice on the practical aspects of screenwriting and mastering Hollywood from a professional. This book will save you time, embarrassment, and frustration and will give you an extra edge in taking on the studio system."
— Christopher Vogler, Author, *The Writer's Journey: Mythic Structure for Writers*, Seminar Leader, former Story Consultant with Fox 2000

"I've been extremely fortunate to have Kathie's insightful advice and constructive criticism on my screenplays. She has been a valued mentor to me. Now, through this wonderful book, she can be your mentor, as well."
— Pamela Wallace, Academy Award Co-Winner, Best Writing, Screenplay Written Directly for the Screen, *Witness*

Kathie Fong Yoneda is an industry veteran, currently under contract to Paramount TV in their Longform Division, and an independent script consultant whose clientele includes several award-winning writers. Kathie also conducts workshops based on *The Script-Selling Game* in the U.S. and Europe.

$14.95, 196 pages | Order # 100RLS | ISBN: 0-941188-44-2

FILM DIRECTING: SHOT BY SHOT
Visualizing from Concept to Screen

Steven D. Katz

Over 150,000 Sold! International best-seller!

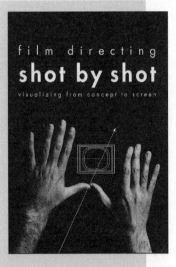

Film Directing: Shot by Shot — with its famous blue cover — is the best-known book on directing and a favorite of professional directors as an on-set quick reference guide.

This international bestseller is a complete catalog of visual techniques and their stylistic implications, enabling working filmmakers to expand their knowledge.

Contains in-depth information on shot composition, staging sequences, visualization tools, framing and composition techniques, camera movement, blocking tracking shots, script analysis, and much more.

Includes over 750 storyboards and illustrations, with never-before-published storyboards from Steven Spielberg's *Empire of the Sun*, Orson Welles' *Citizen Kane*, and Alfred Hitchcock's *The Birds*.

"(To become a director) you have to teach yourself what makes movies good and what makes them bad. John Singleton has been my mentor... he's the one who told me what movies to watch and to read *Shot by Shot*."
— Ice Cube, *New York Times*

"A generous number of photos and superb illustrations accompany each concept, many of the graphics being from Katz' own pen... *Film Directing: Shot by Shot* is a feast for the eyes."
— *Videomaker Magazine*

Steven D. Katz is also the author of *Film Directing: Cinematic Motion*.

$27.95, 366 pages
Order # 7RLS | ISBN: 0-941188-10-8

NEW TITLE

WRITING THE KILLER TREATMENT
Selling Your Story without a Script

Michael Halperin

The most commonly heard phrase in Hollywood is not "Let's do lunch." In reality, the expression you'll most often hear in production, studio, and agency offices is: "Okay, send me a treatment."

A treatment, which may range from one to several dozen pages, is the snapshot of your feature film or TV script. A treatment reveals your story's structure, introduces your characters and hooks, and is often your first and only opportunity to pitch your project.

This is the only book that takes you through the complete process of creating treatments that sell. It includes: developing believable characters and story structure; understanding the distinctions between treatments for screenplays, adaptations, sitcoms, Movies of the Week, episodic television, and soaps; useful exercises that will help you develop your craft as a writer; insightful interviews with Oscar and Emmy winners; tips and query letters for finding an agent and/or a producer; and *What Every Writer Needs to Know*, from the Writers Guild of America, west.

"Michael Halperin's well-crafted book offers a meticulous – and simple – plan for writing your treatment, from its inception to the final polish."
— Sable Jak, *Scr(i)pt Magazine*

Michael Halperin worked as an Executive Story Consultant for 20th Century Fox Television and on staff with Universal Television. He has written and/or produced numerous television episodes. He is the author of *Writing the Second Act: Building Conflict and Tension in Your Film Script*.

$14.95, 171 pages
Order # 97RLS
ISBN: 0-941188-40-X

SETTING UP YOUR SHOTS
Great Camera Moves Every Filmmaker Should Know

Jeremy Vineyard

Written in straightforward, non-technical language and laid out in a nonlinear format with self-contained chapters for quick, on-the-set reference, *Setting Up Your Shots* is like a Swiss army knife for filmmakers! Using examples from over 140 popular films, this book provides detailed descriptions of more than 100 camera setups, angles, and techniques — in an easy-to-use horizontal "wide-screen" format.

Setting Up Your Shots is an excellent primer for beginning filmmakers and students of film theory, as well as a handy guide for working filmmakers. If you are a director, a storyboard artist, or an animator, use this book. It is the culmination of hundreds of hours of research.

Contains 150 references to the great shots from your favorite films, including *2001: A Space Odyssey*, *Blue Velvet*, *The Matrix*, *The Usual Suspects*, and *Vertigo*.

"Perfect for any film enthusiast looking for the secrets behind creating film. Because of its simplicity of design and straightforward storyboards, *Setting Up Your Shots* is destined to be mandatory reading at film schools throughout the world."
— Ross Otterman, *Directed By Magazine*

Jeremy Vineyard is a director and screenwriter who moved to Los Angeles in 1997 to pursue a feature filmmaking career. He has several spec scripts in development.

$19.95, 132 pages
Order # 8RLS
ISBN: 0-941188-73-6

ORDER FORM

MICHAEL WIESE PRODUCTIONS
11288 VENTURA BLVD., # 621
STUDIO CITY, CA 91604
E-MAIL: MWPSALES@MWP.COM
WEB SITE: WWW.MWP.COM

WRITE OR FAX FOR A FREE CATALOG

PLEASE SEND ME THE FOLLOWING BOOKS:

TITLE	ORDER NUMBER (#RLS _____)	AMOUNT
	SHIPPING	
	CALIFORNIA TAX **(8.25%)**	
	TOTAL ENCLOSED	

PLEASE MAKE CHECK OR MONEY ORDER PAYABLE TO:

MICHAEL WIESE PRODUCTIONS

(CHECK ONE) ____ MASTERCARD ____VISA ____AMEX

CREDIT CARD NUMBER _____

EXPIRATION DATE _____

CARDHOLDER'S NAME _____

CARDHOLDER'S SIGNATURE _____

SHIP TO:

NAME _____

ADDRESS _____

CITY _____ STATE _____ ZIP _____

COUNTRY _____ TELEPHONE _____